Claude and Anthropic: the origins of an ethical and revolutionary AI

Grégory G. CORBET

Claude
et
Anthropic

The origins of an ethical and revolutionary AI

Table of Contents

Grégory G. CORBET

Claude
et
Anthropic

The origins of an ethical
and revolutionary AI

Foreword

At the dawn of a new technological era, where artificial intelligence is permeating every aspect of our daily lives, it seems essential to rethink our relationship with these technologies and to consider their development from the perspective of responsibility and ethics. This book presents itself as an in-depth reflection on the evolution of artificial intelligence, with a particular focus on Claude, the language model developed by Anthropic, and on how the latter, as well as the approach of its creator, redefine our relationship with technology.

The rapid advances in AI in recent years have generated both excitement and questions. On the one hand, we are witnessing spectacular innovations capable of transforming working methods, automating complex tasks, and generating content in a near-human manner. On the other, these technologies raise crucial issues related to security, transparency, algorithmic bias, and governance. Anthropic, with its Claude model, stands out for its commitment to developing artificial intelligence that is not only powerful, but also, above all, aligned with essential human values such as responsibility, fairness, and transparency. It is in this context that this book explores the different dimensions of this technological revolution.

This work is aimed at both experts in the field and a wider audience eager to understand how AI is transforming our societies and influencing our lifestyles. We have attempted to combine scientific rigor with accessibility, presenting both the technical foundations of modern language models and the ethical reflections that accompany them. By tracing the historical evolution of artificial intelligence—from Turing's early ideas to current breakthroughs in deep learning—and analyzing the strategies adopted by Anthropic to integrate security and moderation mechanisms into Claude, this book offers a comprehensive view of the current state of AI and its future prospects.

The foreword to this book is also intended as a call for collective reflection. In a world where technology is evolving at breakneck speed, it is essential that researchers, developers, policymakers, and citizens engage in open dialogue about the implications of these innovations. We are convinced that, to be truly beneficial, artificial intelligence must be part of a collaborative approach, incorporating feedback from multiple stakeholders and constantly adapting to societal developments.

Throughout the pages, we will address a variety of topics: the technical challenges of training models, strategies for minimizing bias and reducing the risk of misinformation, the integration of AI into professional environments and the transformation of workflows, as well as avenues for reflection to anticipate future challenges in terms of regulation, competition, and governance. We will also examine how Claude compares to other major language models and how it could influence the transition towards more general and specialized artificial intelligence.

We hope this book will inspire everyone to question the role of technology in our society and to consider the future of AI through an innovative and ethical lens. Whether you are a professional in the sector, a researcher, or simply curious about technological transformations, this book offers you the keys to understanding the complex issues of artificial intelligence and to imagining together a future where these technologies serve the common good.

Welcome to this journey to the heart of responsible AI, a field in perpetual flux, but one that holds immense potential to positively transform our world.

Introduction

We live in an era where artificial intelligence (AI) continues to push the boundaries of what is possible, radically transforming the way we think, work, and interact. At the heart of this technological revolution is Claude, the large language model developed by Anthropic, which embodies a new generation of intelligent tools designed to be both powerful and responsible. This book aims to explore in depth the origins, advances, and future prospects of Claude and Anthropic, while highlighting the ethical, technical, and societal issues that arise from them.

From the earliest theories of artificial intelligence formulated by pioneers like Alan Turing to recent breakthroughs in neural networks and deep learning, the path taken by AI has been fraught with bold innovations and major challenges. The first machines, inspired by the vision of Turing and his contemporaries, were simple computational simulators. Today, thanks to sophisticated architectures like Transformer, language models like Claude are distinguished by their ability to understand, generate, and synthesize human language with unprecedented finesse.

Anthropic stands out in this space by placing safety, ethics, and alignment with human values at the heart of its approach. While many players focus primarily on accelerating performance, Anthropic has chosen to invest in research that aims not only to push technical boundaries, but also to ensure that these technologies serve the common good. The so-called "Constitutional AI" approach is a striking example: it is a set of guiding principles that guide the behavior of models to avoid the generation of harmful content, limit bias, and promote transparency in the use of AI.

In this book, we offer a detailed exploration of several key dimensions shaping the future of AI. We begin by reviewing the history of artificial intelligence, tracing the crucial shift from symbolism to neural networks and explaining how technical breakthroughs, such as the backpropagation algorithm and the Transformer architecture, enabled the creation of systems capable of processing massive amounts of data and generating remarkably accurate answers. We then discuss the role of major players in this evolution, from academic pioneers to major technology companies, and highlight the birth of Anthropic, a company founded by experts who wanted to rethink AI with a view to accountability and transparency.

We will also examine how Claude fits into the landscape of large language models. Compared to systems such as OpenAI's GPT or Google's BERT, Claude stands out not only for its performance, but also for its specific approach to alignment and moderation, aimed at providing safe and balanced answers. Technical challenges, such as training optimization, bias management, or maintaining context over long conversations, will be analyzed in detail to understand the innovations implemented by Anthropic.

Additionally, the book will explore Claude's real-world applications in a variety of industries—customer service, editorial, education, healthcare, law, and finance—and illustrate how AI is transforming business workflows by automating repetitive tasks, improving efficiency, and freeing up time to focus on high-value activities. We'll also explore how integrating Claude through APIs and collaborations with other technology tools is fostering smooth, incremental adoption across diverse environments.

The book will finally focus on forward-looking reflections on the future of responsible AI. In a constantly evolving world, anticipating new challenges—regulatory, competitive, ethical, and governance—appears to be imperative to ensure that artificial intelligence technologies are deployed securely and beneficially for society. Debates on shared governance, algorithmic transparency, and the involvement of the scientific community and the general public will illustrate the importance of open and participatory dialogue in building a global framework for AI.

This book is intended to be both a dive into history and technology, and a reflection on the societal impact of artificial intelligence. It invites the reader to understand how innovations such as Claude's transform not only the technologies we use, but also our way of seeing the world, laying the foundations for a future where AI serves humans in a transparent, ethical, and responsible manner.

Chapter 1: Genesis of AI Research

Historical context: the first artificial intelligence programs and the major stages of research.

1. The beginnings of thinking about artificial intelligence

1.1. Conceptual foundations: the Turing machine and the question of mechanical thinking

- **Alan Turing (1912-1954)** , British mathematician, is considered one of the founding fathers of computer science and AI.

- His work on the "□Turing machine□» (1936) established the fundamental principles of automated calculation , showing that a universal machine could, in theory , execute any algorithmic calculation.

- In 1950, Turing published the article "□Computing Machinery and Intelligence□" , in which he asks the famous question "□Can machines think?□?□" and proposes a protocol for evaluating the intelligence of a machine□: the **Turing Test** .

    o The idea is to subject an interrogator to a simultaneous written discussion with two entities (one human, one machine) without knowing which is which. If the interrogator cannot distinguish the machine from the human, the machine is considered to have passed the test.

- Although the Turing Question remains controversial and debated, it marked a conceptual turning point by bringing to light the notion that a computer program could mimic (or even reproduce) certain aspects of human thought.

1.2. The first cybernetic reflections

- In the 1940s and 1950s, **cybernetics** (Norbert Wiener, John von Neumann, Warren McCulloch, etc.) studied feedback loops and the regulation of machines, often drawing inspiration from the functioning of the brain.

- This interdisciplinary research (biology, mathematics, engineering) lays the foundations of **control theory** and automation , paving the way for systems capable of adjusting their behavior.

---

2. The official birth of AI: the Dartmouth conference (1956)

2.1. The founding research project

- **John McCarthy** , **Marvin Minsky** , **Claude Shannon** and **Nathan Rochester** organized a summer seminar in Dartmouth, USA, which historically marked the official birth of artificial intelligence as an autonomous scientific discipline.

- The founding idea is to propose that all aspects of learning and intelligence can, in principle, be described precisely enough to be simulated by a machine.

- This seminar brought together other big names such as Allen Newell and Herbert A. Simon, who already presented innovative programs such as "☐Logic Theorist☐» (software capable of proving theorems in logic) .

2.2. Hope for a quick resolution

- The founders of AI were very optimistic☐: they believed that achieving human - like artificial intelligence was a matter of decades , or even years .

- During this period, many university laboratories and research centers were created, notably at MIT (with Marvin Minsky), Stanford (with John McCarthy) and Carnegie Mellon (with Newell and Simon).

---

3. The first programs and symbolic approaches

3.1. The Logic Theorist (1956)

- Developed by Allen Newell, Herbert A. Simon, and Cliff Shaw, **Logic Theorist** is often considered one of the first artificial intelligence programs.

- It had the ability to automatically prove theorems of formal logic, including some from Russell and Whitehead's Principia Mathematica.

- This achievement showed that some tasks considered intelligent could be formalized in the form of logical rules and solved by a computer.

3.2. The General Problem Solver (GPS) (1957)

- Also created by Newell and Simon, the **General Problem Solver** aimed to provide a generic framework for solving different types of problems by reducing them to logical steps (initial states, final states, intermediate operations).

- Although promising on paper, the system quickly ran into computational limitations when faced with complex problems (which would later characterize the challenges of symbolic AI).

3.3. Expert systems and the symbolic approach

- In the 1960s and 1970s, AI focused primarily on so-called **symbolic** or **knowledge-based methods** .

  - Human knowledge is formalized in the form of rules, facts, concepts, logic.

- o **Expert systems** are the most successful example of this approach.☐: they seek to encapsulate the expertise of a particular field (medicine , geology , etc.) by expressing it in a rule base .

- Famous example☐: **MYCIN** (1970s), an expert system for diagnosing infectious diseases and recommending antibiotic treatments.

---

4. The rise of neural networks and the emergence of the connectionist approach

4.1. The perceptron (1957)

- **Frank Rosenblatt** proposed a model of artificial neural network called **the Perceptron** . Inspired by the biological neuron, it is a basic unit capable of learning to classify simple data based on weighted inputs.

- The perceptron had some success (e.g., basic pattern recognition), but it had significant limitations (e.g. , inability to solve the **XOR problem**).

4.2. The book Perceptrons (1969) and the first "AI winter"

- In 1969, **Marvin Minsky** and **Seymour Papert** published a book titled *Perceptrons* , in which they outlined the fundamental limitations of the simple perceptron.

- This book has been (mis)interpreted as proof of the general ineffectiveness of neural networks, helping to divert public and private research away from this approach.

- Therefore, funding is refocusing on symbolic AI, leading to a first "☐AI winter☐» in the field of neural networks (1970s) .

4.3. The revival of connectionism (1980s)

- In the 1980s, new work (e.g., **Rumelhart, Hinton** , and Williams) popularized **gradient backpropagation learning** , allowing training of **multi-layer networks** .

- This advancement opened the way to what is called **deep learning** , although the architectures of the time remained limited by the available computing power and the quantity of data.

---

5. "AI Winters" and Renewed Enthusiasm

5.1. Cycles of promises and disillusionment

- AI has gone through several periods of **intense hope** followed by **disillusionment** and funding cuts.

- The **first winter** (1970s) is linked to the limits of symbolic AI and the ALPAC report (1966) which judged the progress of machine translation to be unconvincing.

- The **second winter** (late 1980s, early 1990s) is linked to the failure of the "□fifth generation of computing□» (in Japan) and at the end of expert systems (when expectations far exceeded reality) .

5.2. Factors of renewal

- Each time, new ideas and new technologies have revived enthusiasm for AI, whether through **connectionism** or through more advanced symbolic techniques (case-based reasoning, genetic algorithms, etc.).

- The arrival of the Internet, the explosion in the amount of digital data and the exponential increase in computing power (Moore's Law) have ended up providing extremely fertile ground for the emergence of **deep learning** .

---

6. The advent of deep learning (2010s)

6.1. Breakthroughs in image recognition and speech recognition

- The early 2010s saw spectacular progress in **computer vision** thanks to **deep neural networks** (AlexNet, 2012).

- The use of large databases (ImageNet, etc.) and GPUs for training has made it possible to significantly exceed the performance of previous approaches.

- In speech recognition, advances by companies like Google, Baidu, and Microsoft have shown that deeper neural networks (DNNs) perform significantly better than approaches based on hidden Markov statistical models.

6.2. Natural language processing (NLP) and large language models

- From the second half of the 2010s, natural language processing underwent a revolution with the introduction of **transformers** (article "□Attention is All You Need□" , 2017, by Vaswani et al.).

- OpenAI's Generative Pre-trained Transformer (GPT) or Google's BERT models have demonstrated the power of **self-supervised learning** on huge corpora of texts, leading to advances in language understanding and generation.

- This approach has served as the basis for many developments, including Claude (Anthropic), ChatGPT (OpenAI), and other major language models.

7. The major stages of AI: a chronological summary

1. **1936-1950** : Preliminary reflection (Turing, cybernetics), notion of universal calculation.

2. **1956** : Dartmouth Conference, official birth of AI.

3. **1956-1970** : Symbolic AI and rule-based systems (Logic Theorist, GPS), first successes but calculation limits.

4. **1957-1969** : Emergence of the perceptron, then criticism (book *Perceptrons*), leading to a disinterest in neural networks.

5. **1970s** : First winters of AI, slowdown in funding, but development of expert systems.

6. **1980s** : Return of connectionism thanks to backpropagation, second wave of research on neural networks.

7. **Late 1980s – 1990s** : Second AI winter, expert systems crisis and failure of the Japanese fifth generation.

8. **2000s** : Rise of the Internet, capitalization on vast databases, hardware acceleration (GPU).

9. **2010 – 2012** : "☐Renaissance☐» deep learning (AlexNet), breakthroughs in image recognition , then in voice recognition.

10. **2017 – present** : Transformer innovation, expansion of large language models (GPT, BERT, Claude, etc.), generative AI (GPT-3, GPT-4, DALL-E, etc.), exponential growth of capabilities and uses.

8. Conclusion: a long road, full of twists and turns

The historical journey of AI is characterized by phases of enthusiasm, followed by moments of skepticism and reduced funding. Each□AI winter□» nevertheless served as a period of questioning and preparation for future technological breakthroughs. Today , with the available computing power, the explosion of data and the advent of revolutionary architectures like transformers , AI is experiencing a period of unprecedented expansion and innovation .

This historical context is essential to understand:

- The conceptual foundations (from Turing onwards) which paved the way for the simulation of cognitive processes.

- The main research trends (symbolic vs. connectionist).

- The success factors (computing power, algorithmic advances, massive data) that have led to current exploits, such as those achieved by Anthropic with Claude, or by other major AI research laboratories.

In short, AI is not a sudden phenomenon.□: it results from decades of discoveries and feedback , which have made it possible to gradually build the impressive range of artificial intelligence applications that we know today .

Emergence of neural networks and deep learning.

1. Foundations and first tracks (1940s-1960s)

1.1. Biological inspirations

- The idea of drawing inspiration from the brain to create an "intelligent" machine was born with **cybernetics** (Norbert Wiener) and **neurophysiology** (Warren McCulloch, Walter Pitts).

- In a 1943 article, McCulloch and Pitts introduced the concept of the "formal neuron": a schematic mathematical model inspired by the biological neuron.

- They thus demonstrate that a formal neural network could, in principle, perform elementary logical operations, laying the foundations for neural modeling for computation.

1.2. Frank Rosenblatt's perceptron (late 1950s)

- **Frank Rosenblatt** proposed the **Perceptron** in 1957: it is a machine capable of learning to classify simple data (for example, distinguishing two shapes) by adjusting the weights associated with neurons.

- Initial tests, funded by the US Navy, showed the perceptron's relative ability to extract relevant features from visual data.

- Rosenblatt predicted that these networks could lead to near-human forms of intelligence. This prediction proved premature, but it helped popularize the idea that neural systems could "learn" from examples.

---

2. The Halt: "Perceptrons" and the First Winter of AI (1969-1970)

2.1. Minsky and Papert's critical analysis

- In 1969, **Marvin Minsky** and **Seymour Papert** published *Perceptrons* , a book that highlighted the limitations of the simple perceptron.

- In particular, they demonstrate that a single-layer perceptron could not solve certain elementary classification problems (e.g., the famous "XOR problem"), due to its inability to model non-linear relationships.

2.2. Consequences: Reduction of funding for neural networks

- The overly broad interpretation of *Perceptrons* has led to the belief that any form of neural approach is doomed to failure.

- Funding agencies and university laboratories then turned away from neural networks in favor of symbolic AI (knowledge representation, expert systems, etc.).

- This period, marked by budget cuts, is commonly referred to as the **first AI winter** .

3. The connectionist revival: backpropagation (1980s)

3.1. Rediscovery of gradient and multilayer networks

- In the 1980s, several researchers (including **Geoffrey Hinton** , **David Rumelhart** , **Ronald Williams** , **Yann LeCun** , **John Hopfield**) demonstrated that it was possible to train **multi-layer neural networks** using the **gradient backpropagation algorithm** .

- The theoretical idea existed as early as the 1960s and 1970s, but it had been little explored. Advances in computing and the introduction of new mathematical perspectives are finally making it possible to partially overcome the limitations of simple perceptrons.

3.2. Key works

- **Rumelhart, Hinton, and Williams (1986)** publish a series of works explaining how backpropagation can correct the weights of the cascaded network, layer by layer.

- Neural networks have proven capable of solving complex problems (recognition of handwritten characters, classification of signals, etc.).

- **John Hopfield** introduces "Hopfield networks" (recurrent, bidirectional) that memorize and recognize patterns.

- In the mid-1980s, enthusiasm for **connectionism** resumed, even though computing infrastructures remained limited.

3.3. Hidden layer systems and multi-layer perceptron (MLP) models

- With "multi-layer perceptrons" comprising **one or more hidden layers** , it becomes possible to learn complex non-linear functions.

- Regularization, normalization, and weight initialization techniques are gradually emerging, improving learning stability.

- Despite these advances, deep neural networks (with many layers) remain difficult to train at large scale due to **vanishing gradient problems** (gradients that cancel out or explode across layers).

---

4. The arrival of "deep networks" and the deep learning revolution (2000s-2010s)

4.1. The role of computing power and data

- From the 2000s onwards, several factors came together:

1. **Explosion of the Internet** and massive generation of data available for learning.

2. **Considerable increase in computing power** , notably thanks to the use of **GPUs** (graphics processors) in training neural networks.

3. Emergence of more sophisticated neural architectures and techniques for deep training (better initializations, normalization layers, etc.).

4.2. The pioneering work of Hinton, Bengio and LeCun

- **Geoffrey Hinton** , **Yoshua Bengio** and **Yann LeCun** , often considered the "fathers of modern deep learning", develop methods to train **deep networks** (multiple layers) with layer-by-layer pre-training techniques (RBM, stacked autoencoders, etc.).

- These approaches allow for better initialization of weights and avoid gradients vanishing in deep layers.

- We quickly see that the more we increase the depth of the network (and the size of the data sets), the better the performance.

4.3. The AlexNet "bomb" (2012)

- In 2012, **Alex Krizhevsky** , **Ilya Sutskever** , and Geoffrey Hinton won the **ImageNet competition** using a **deep convolutional network** (CNN) called **AlexNet** .

- Their result far exceeds traditional computer vision approaches (SVM, "hand-made" features, etc.).

- AlexNet is distinguished by its intensive use of GPUs for training, regularization techniques (dropout), and a deeper network design than previous CNNs.

- This victory is considered the catalyst for the deep learning revolution in computer vision.

5. Advances in vision, speech recognition and language processing (2010s)

5.1. Image recognition: from VGGNet to ResNet

- After AlexNet, other convolutional architectures are coming: **VGGNet** (Oxford, 2014), **GoogLeNet/Inception** (Google, 2014-2015) and especially **ResNet** (Microsoft, 2015).

- **ResNet** (He, Zhang, Ren, Sun) introduces "skip connections", avoiding gradient loss in very deep networks (up to more than 100 layers).

- CNNs are becoming the standard in computer vision, providing unparalleled performance for classification, object detection, semantic segmentation, and more.

5.2. Speech recognition and signal processing

- The same principles of **deep neural networks** (DNNs) are extremely effective for **speech recognition** .

- Major technology players (Google, Microsoft, Baidu, Amazon, Apple) are adopting these architectures for their virtual assistants and oral translation services.

- Recurrent models (LSTM, GRU) specialize in processing temporal sequences (audio signal, time series), significantly improving recognition rates compared to previous statistical models (HMM, GMM).

5.3. Natural Language Processing and Introduction of Transformers

- Until 2017, **NLP** (Natural Language Processing) relied heavily on recurrent networks (LSTM) and attention mechanisms (seq2seq).

- The publication of the article **"Attention is All You Need" (Vaswani et al., 2017) introduces the Transformer** architecture , which relies solely on self-attention mechanisms, avoiding recursion.

- The Transformer drastically reduces the difficulty of parallelizing training and achieves excellent performance on translation, summarization, and text understanding tasks.

- This new paradigm will open the door to **large language models** (GPT, BERT, T5, etc.) and literally transform the field of NLP and text generation.

---

6. Massive expansion and large language models (2020s)

6.1. The emergence of very large models

- As computing capacity (GPUs, TPUs, etc.) and access to data explode, industrial and academic research labs are developing **gigantic neural models** , reaching tens or even hundreds of billions of parameters.

- **OpenAI Launches GPT** (Generative Pre-trained Transformer) Series□: GPT-2 (2019), GPT-3 (2020), GPT-4 (2023), showing that with a Transformer architecture and self - supervised pre -training on huge corpora , we obtain impressive language generation and understanding capabilities .

- **Google** and other companies are following the same approach with BERT, T5, PaLM, etc.

6.2. Areas of application: a meteoric rise

- Chatbots capable of fluid dialogue, ultra-sophisticated **virtual assistants ,** almost human-like **automatic translation , and text creation** (blog posts, articles, computer code) have become realities accessible to the general public.

- In computer vision, GANs (Generative Adversarial Networks), then **diffusion models** (Stable Diffusion, DALL-E, Midjourney) make it possible to generate high-quality images from simple text descriptions.

6.3. Towards an explosion of the sectors concerned

- Industry, health, finance, transportation, education, artistic creation: practically all fields integrate deep learning solutions to automate tasks, analyze large volumes of data, or generate new content.

- Questions of **ethics** , algorithmic **bias** , **energy consumption** and **regulation** then emerge as major challenges in the field, as does the pursuit of performance and precision.

---

7. Current challenges and future prospects

7.1. The problems of deep learning

- **Data labeling** : Despite the rise of self-supervision, many tasks still require annotated data that is expensive to produce.

- **Data bias and robustness** : Neural networks learn biases present in training data, leading to unintentional discriminations or errors in real-life situations.

- **Explainability** : Understanding the decisions of a deep network remains a major challenge. Toolboxes (Grad-CAM, LIME, SHAP, etc.) attempt to provide insights, but complete transparency is still a long way off.

7.2. Towards new hybrid architectures?

- Some researchers are exploring the combination of **symbolic AI** and **deep learning** , seeking to reconcile the generalization power of neural networks with the logical reasoning and abstraction capacity of knowledge systems.

- The use of differentiable memory mechanisms, neurosymbolic architectures or **prompt engineering** (in the case of large language models) suggests ways to overcome the current limitations of deep learning.

7.3. The horizon of general AI (AGI)

- The spectacular performance of deep learning is sparking debates about the possibility of **artificial general intelligence** (AGI).

- Some argue that deep neural networks, coupled with emerging techniques, could approach human cognitive abilities. Others argue that radically new conceptual breakthroughs will be required.

- In any case, the rise of deep learning has permanently changed the face of computing and artificial intelligence research, opening the way to new applications that were unimaginable just a few years ago.

8. Conclusion

The emergence of neural networks and deep learning is the result of a long historical journey, punctuated by fundamental discoveries (the perceptron, backpropagation, CNNs, Transformers) and punctuated by AI "winters" when funding or trust dried up.

It was only truly with the rise of computing hardware, the abundance of data, and the development of new architectures that deep learning established itself as a pillar of modern AI. Today, deep neural networks have established themselves in almost all fields related to perception, language, or decision-making, and continue to evolve at high speed. The boundaries of what is possible are pushed back almost every year, revealing technological, economic, and societal perspectives of unprecedented magnitude, while raising essential ethical and governance questions.

The major players who shaped the field of AI before the creation of Anthropic.

1. Individual Pioneers

1.1. Alan Turing (1912-1954)

- Considered one of the fathers of modern computing.
- In 1936, he proposed the concept of the **Turing machine** , which formalized the notion of universal computation.
- In his 1950 article " **Computing Machinery and Intelligence** ," he asked the question " **Can machines think?** " and described the **Turing Test** , which was supposed to assess whether a machine's conversation was indistinguishable from that of a human.
- His ideas profoundly influenced thinking about the possibility of mechanized intelligence, paving the way for AI.

1.2. John McCarthy (1927-2011)

- Computer scientist who coined the term **"Artificial Intelligence"** (conceived for the 1956 Dartmouth conference).
- Creator of the **Lisp language** (1958), which would become one of the leading languages for AI research, particularly for symbol manipulation and writing expert systems.
- Co-founder of the **Stanford Artificial Intelligence Laboratory (SAIL)** , he played a central role in the expansion of symbolic AI.

1.3. Marvin Minsky (1927-2016)

- Influential researcher at **MIT** (Massachusetts Institute of Technology), co-founder of the **MIT AI Lab** .

- Major contributor to theories of symbolic AI and to thinking around human and artificial intelligence.
- His book **Perceptrons** (1969, with Seymour Papert) temporarily halted research into neural networks, but he remained a key figure, notably defending the idea that knowledge could be decomposed into cognitive agents (see his work *The Society of Mind*).

1.4. Herbert A. Simon (1916-2001) and Allen Newell (1927-1992)

- Major research duo at **Carnegie Mellon University (CMU)**.
- Creators of seminal programs such as **Logic Theorist** (1956) and **General Problem Solver (GPS)** (1957).
- They demonstrated that problem solving and reasoning could be formalized as logical rules.
- Simon, Nobel Prize winner in Economics (1978), has profoundly influenced decision theory and cognitive psychology, thus linking AI to various disciplines.

1.5. Claude Shannon (1916-2001)

- "Father of information theory".
- Present at the Dartmouth conference, he contributed to the formulation of founding ideas about AI, notably the study of problem solving (strategy games like chess).
- His work on information has greatly influenced the field of cybernetics and communications, essential foundations for the later development of AI.

1.6. Seymour Papert (1928-2016)

- Collaborator of Marvin Minsky at MIT.
- Co-author of the book *Perceptrons* .
- One of the pioneers of the constructivist approach to education, creator of the **Logo language** , aimed at teaching programming and logic to children.

- His ideas on computer learning have had a considerable impact on the pedagogical approach to AI.

1.7. Edward Feigenbaum (born 1936)

- A leading figure in the design of **expert systems** in the 1970s.
- Known for the DENDRAL (diagnostics in organic chemistry) and MYCIN (medical diagnostics) projects, demonstrating the power of expert rules coded within computer programs.

1.8. Judea Pearl (born 1936)

- Computer scientist and philosopher, pioneer in the field of **probabilistic reasoning** and **Bayesian networks** .
- His work (notably his book *Probabilistic Reasoning in Intelligent Systems* , 1988) revolutionized the way AI systems handle uncertainty, paving the way for more robust decision models.

1.9. Deep learning pioneers: Geoff Hinton, Yann LeCun, Yoshua Bengio

- **Geoffrey Hinton** : rediscoverer and popularizer of **gradient backpropagation** in the 1980s, and a central figure behind modern deep learning (notably AlexNet, 2012).
- **Yann LeCun** : Designer of the first **convolutional networks** (LeNet) applied to reading handwritten numbers. Later became Director of AI at Meta (Facebook).
- **Yoshua Bengio** : Researcher at the University of Montreal, developed advanced methods for autoencoders and generative models and contributed to the deep learning community through the MILA (Montreal Institute for Learning Algorithms).

2. Historical universities and laboratories

2.1. MIT AI Lab

- Founded notably by Marvin Minsky and John McCarthy.
- Cradle of many AI projects, both symbolic and practical.
- Place of emergence of key computer languages and tools (Lisp Machines, etc.).
- Has produced many notable figures in AI and has forged close ties with the industry.

2.2. Stanford AI Lab (SAIL)

- Co-founded by John McCarthy after his departure from MIT.
- Known for his work in **robotics** , **automatic reasoning** and **expert systems** (MYCIN, etc.).
- Also played an important role in training Silicon Valley entrepreneurs and researchers.

2.3. Carnegie Mellon University (CMU)

- A leading center of AI research thanks to the initial collaboration between Herbert A. Simon and Allen Newell.
- Has contributed to **cognitive science** , **robotics** , **machine learning** , and **symbolic reasoning** .
- Great pioneers (Raj Reddy, Takeo Kanade, etc.) have developed innovations in voice recognition and computer vision there.

2.4. University of Edinburgh and other European centres

- In Europe, institutions like **the University of Edinburgh** have played a key role in computational linguistics and logical reasoning.
- The development of **Prolog** (at the University of Marseille, then Edinburgh) provided a basis for logic programming and rule-based systems.

3. Leading technology companies

3.1. IBM

- A historic player in IT, IBM supported AI research from the 1950s and 1960s.
- Their project **Deep Blue** (1997) made a name for itself by defeating world chess champion Garry Kasparov.
- Later, the creation of **Watson** (winner of Jeopardy! in 2011) illustrated the scaling up of AI systems in language processing and data analysis.

3.2. Microsoft

- Very early involved in research in AI and language processing (thanks to Microsoft Research, founded in the 1990s).
- Invested in speech recognition, computer vision and multiple academic collaborations.
- His work, and his partnerships (with OpenAI from 2019), have contributed to the massive dissemination of neural approaches.

3.3. Google (and Google Brain)

- Google, through the acquisition of **DeepMind** (founded in London in 2010 by Demis Hassabis, Shane Legg and Mustafa Suleyman), has become a major player in **deep**

reinforcement learning (with the success of AlphaGo in 2016).
- **Google Brain** initiative (led by Jeff Dean and Andrew Ng, among others) has pushed research into deep neural networks (particularly for machine translation, vision, and Transformer-type architectures).
- The emergence of **TensorFlow** provided a popular open-source framework that standardized the development of deep learning models.

3.4. Facebook (Meta)

- Within **Facebook AI Research (FAIR)** , under the leadership of Yann LeCun, Meta has invested heavily in computer vision, NLP and recommendation models.
- Advances in open source FAIR (PyTorch, the first version of which also comes from Facebook) have contributed to the growth of the deep learning community.

3.5. OpenAI

- Founded in 2015 by a group including Elon Musk, Sam Altman, Ilya Sutskever, Greg Brockman, etc.
- Before Anthropic, OpenAI played a crucial role in the proliferation of **large language models** (GPT-2, GPT-3, GPT-4) and in raising public awareness of the capabilities and limitations of generative AI.

---

4. Public and private financing bodies

4.1. DARPA (United States)

- The U.S. Defense Research Agency (DARPA) has financially supported multiple AI projects since the 1960s.

- **Speech Understanding Research (SUR)** program in the 1970s led to major advances in speech recognition.
- DARPA has also funded exploratory projects in robotics, autonomous vehicles (Grand Challenge), and computer vision.

4.2. Government programs abroad

- In the 1980s, the Japanese and European governments launched major projects (Fifth Generation Computing in Japan, ESPRIT Program in Europe) around microelectronics and AI.
- Despite results that sometimes fell short of expectations, these initiatives paved the way for future research.

4.3. Foundations and major conferences

- Foundations such as the American **National Science Foundation (NSF) and the Alfred P. Sloan Foundation** have helped support basic research.
- The major specialized conferences (IJCAI, AAAI, NeurIPS, ICML, ACL, etc.) have become institutionalized over the decades, serving as a meeting place and emulation for the international scientific community.

5. Major research trends before Anthropic

5.1. Symbolic AI (1950s to 1980s)

- Based on the representation of knowledge in the form of rules and symbols (logic, expert systems).
- Contributes to problem solving, automatic theorem proving, medical diagnostic systems (MYCIN) and planning.

5.2. The connectionist approach (neural networks)

- Started with the perceptron (Rosenblatt), put on hold after *Perceptrons* (1969), relaunched in the 1980s thanks to backpropagation (Hinton, Rumelhart, LeCun).
- **Deep learning** " became widespread in the 2000s, with the explosion of computing power and data.

5.3. Probabilistic methods and uncertain reasoning

- Led by Judea Pearl and others, they rely on **Bayesian networks** , **statistical inference** and "classical" **machine learning** (SVM, decision trees, etc.).
- Foundational elements for the robustness of AI in complex and uncertain environments.

5.4. The advent of Transformers and generative AI (2017-2020)

- "Attention is All You Need" (2017) revolutionizes natural language processing.
- OpenAI and other labs are demonstrating the power of **large language models** (GPT, BERT, etc.).
- Just before the creation of Anthropic (2021), this technology became widespread, raising many ethical and AI governance questions.

---

6. Synthesis: a multidisciplinary heritage

Before Anthropic, AI research was shaped by:

1. **Visionary individuals** (Turing, McCarthy, Minsky, Simon, Pearl, etc.) who defined the conceptual, mathematical and ethical foundations of AI.

2. **Historic university laboratories** (MIT, Stanford, CMU) which have structured teaching and research in the field, training several generations of scientists and engineers.
3. **Technology companies** (IBM, Microsoft, Google, Facebook, OpenAI) that have provided financial resources, computing capacity and industrial applications, popularizing AI among the general public.
4. **Public agencies** (DARPA, NSF, national programs) and private foundations, whose funding has supported both theoretical research and practical demonstrations.
5. **An international community of researchers** , meeting around major conferences and scholarly associations, guaranteeing the exchange of ideas and the dynamism of the field.

It is in this rich heritage, woven with controversies, spectacular advances and ethical challenges, that Anthropic has come to inscribe itself, drawing on the tradition of cutting-edge research and adding its own vision around security , **ethics and** responsibility in **the** development of artificial intelligence models.

Chapter 2: Foundations and Mission of Anthropic

Presentation of the founders and their background.

1. The context of the founding of Anthropic

Anthropic was founded in early 2021 by former members of OpenAI. The stated goal was to build an organization focused specifically on the **safety** , ethics **,** and **responsibility** of artificial intelligence, while continuing research on large language models and advanced AI systems.

Anthropic's founders, for the most part, have acquired solid technical and managerial experience in leading organizations (notably OpenAI) and decided to bring these skills to a new entity, with its own corporate culture and a focus on **long-term research** and AI **safety .**

---

2. Dario Amodei: CEO and Co-Founder

2.1. Academic background and initial experiences

- Dario Amodei is one of the central scientific figures in Anthropic.
- He holds a PhD in biophysics from Stanford University. His initial training combines physics , biology **and** mathematics , giving him a multidisciplinary profile.
- His interest gradually shifted towards machine learning, AI, and more specifically large language models.

2.2. Role at OpenAI

- Before co-founding Anthropic, Dario Amodei was Vice President of Research at **OpenAI** .
- In particular, he has supervised or contributed closely to the organization's flagship projects, including work relating to AI safety and the training of large language models (the different iterations of GPT for example).
- His role was to supervise the research teams, define strategic directions on both technical and ethical issues, and ensure the performance of the models.

2.3. Motivations for creating Anthropic

- Over time, Dario Amodei has become increasingly concerned about the **security** and **control issues** surrounding powerful AI.
- He and other collaborators chose to create a separate entity, where research on AI **safety could be central and where issues of governance and transparency would be integrated from the design of the models.**
- Since Anthropic's founding, he has been its CEO, overseeing the scientific and strategic direction of the company.

3. Daniela Amodei: President and Co-founder

3.1. Background and skills

- Daniela Amodei is the sister of Dario Amodei and another key figure in Anthropic.
- His background, more oriented towards **political science** , **communication** and **management** , allows him to bring a different perspective to the project.
- She also worked at OpenAI before joining the Anthropic adventure, holding positions related to **strategy** , **team coordination** and **communication** .

3.2. Organizational role

- As President of Anthropic, Daniela Amodei oversees the company's operations, internal and external relations, and corporate culture.
- It emphasizes ethics , social **responsibility** and **transparent communication** , fundamental points for an organization dedicated to developing powerful and potentially sensitive AI systems.
- Daniela also participates in defining the **funding strategy** and the research roadmap, working closely with Dario Amodei.

---

4. Jack Clark: Co-founder and AI public policy expert

4.1. Professional context

- Jack Clark was previously **Director of Policy** at OpenAI.
- His role was to assess the potential impacts of AI on society, engage with government institutions, and contribute to the development of safety and ethics standards.
- His experience in technical journalism (he notably wrote for Bloomberg) has allowed him to develop skills in popularizing and putting into perspective advances in AI.

4.2. Involvement in Anthropic

- At Anthropic, Jack Clark focuses on the **policy** , **regulatory** , and **governance aspects** of AI.
- His presence underlines Anthropic's desire to integrate these dimensions into its strategic orientations and research from an early stage.

- Issues of transparency, accountability and public communication around AI remain one of his key concerns.

---

5. Other co-founders and key members

5.1. Varied scientific and technical profiles

- Alongside Dario and Daniela Amodei, as well as Jack Clark, Anthropic has other co-founders and major researchers, often from OpenAI or other major institutions (prestigious universities, research laboratories).
- Many of them have a solid background in **mathematics** , **physics** , **computer science** or even **machine learning** , having published in major conferences (NeurIPS, ICML, etc.).

5.2. A complementarity of skills

- The founding team includes not only scientists, but also specialized profiles in **product management** , **IT security** , **public policy** , **law** , etc.
- This multidisciplinary approach is in line with Anthropic's logic: to study and develop extremely powerful AI systems, it is essential to bring together different areas of expertise (technical, ethical, legal, etc.).

---

6. Common philosophy and shared vision

6.1. Focus on AI "security" and "alignment"

- Since its inception, Anthropic has focused on the concept of **alignment** : how to ensure that AI models truly reflect human values and intentions, and do not generate undesirable consequences.
- The founders, drawing on their experience at OpenAI, wanted to create a structure where these questions would be at the very heart of R&D and not simply an "add-on" at the end of the chain.

6.2. Open but cautious research

- Anthropic is positioning itself in line with the "open" approach to AI, by publishing part of its research in scientific journals and making certain tools or preprints available.
- Nevertheless, the company remains attentive to **risk management** : transparency is desired, but without ignoring the security problems potentially linked to the uncontrolled distribution of overly powerful models.

6.3. The role of corporate culture

- Daniela Amodei, in particular, is working to establish a corporate culture that values collaboration, the consideration of ethical issues at all levels, and cooperation with other players in the sector (universities, NGOs, etc.).
- The founders believe that **international cooperation** and the **exchange of best practices** are crucial to ensure responsible development of AI.

7. Conclusion

Anthropic's founders, mainly from OpenAI (Dario and Daniela Amodei, Jack Clark, etc.), have significant experience in the field of **large language models** , **AI safety research** and

public policy .

Their shared desire, fueled by their backgrounds and reflections, is to build an entity focused on the **safety** , **responsibility** and **effectiveness** of AI, pushing the boundaries of research while remaining aware of ethical and societal issues.

This vision is being realized today through Anthropic's work on alignment **, bias** reduction , advanced understanding of AI **behavior** and the exploration of new approaches for more robust and better controlled models.

Vision, values and ethics at the origin of Anthropic.

1. Background: The need for AI focused on safety and ethics

1.1. The urgency of addressing the risks associated with large models

- As **deep learning techniques** and large language models have advanced, the **potential risks** associated with these powerful AIs have become more evident (misinformation, bias, lack of transparency).
- The founders of Anthropic, when leaving OpenAI, wanted to build a structure where the issue of **security** and alignment (alignment of models with human values) would not be relegated to the background, but would become the very **heart** of the research strategy.

1.2. Values already present among the founders

- Dario Amodei, for example, had conducted extensive research at OpenAI on AI safety, publishing several works on **preventing unexpected behaviors** and "biases" that could emerge in models.
- The other co-founders (e.g. Jack Clark, Daniela Amodei) shared the belief that the AI field required more transparent **governance** and an **ethical approach** that took into account societal impacts.

---

2. Anthropic's vision: AI serving the common good

2.1. Promoting "long-termism"

- Anthropic is part of a school of thought often called "**long-termism** ," which involves integrating **the long-term consequences** of innovations, rather than limiting itself to immediate benefits.
- In this perspective, we consider not only the commercial or practical use of AI, but also the negative externalities, **potential abuses** and the influence of intelligent systems on society in several years or decades.

2.2. Making safety a founding pillar

- Unlike some companies focused primarily on **performance** or accelerating **ever** -larger models, Anthropic emphasizes **reliability** , **security** , and **explainability** .
- Their vision is that the **robustness** of a model, its **integrity** , and its **ability to respect ethical constraints** (notably by avoiding hate speech or limiting the spread of dangerous content) are as important as pure technological innovation.

2.3. Building a Trusted AI

- One of Anthropic's major goals is to **gain the trust of the public** and users.
- They are working on concepts like AI **alignment** (aligning the goals of AI with those of human society) and AI **interpretability** (understanding how and why a model makes certain decisions).
- This is to ensure that, as models gain power, they remain under **human control** and do not deviate from accepted norms (ethical, legal, cultural, etc.).

3. The values at the heart of Anthropic

3.1. Responsibility and prudence

- **responsible** " approach to research , which involves continuously assessing the **risks** associated with the publication of new models or new discoveries.
- The company wants to avoid past mistakes (for example, the uncontrolled spread of AI technologies that could generate misinformation or be exploited maliciously).
- This **caution** is evident in how Anthropic shares or does not share its work: they seek to advance research while weighing the consequences of each publication.

3.2. Transparency and accountability

- Although security is paramount, Anthropic does not intend to operate clandestinely **or** withhold information: they advocate " **reasoned transparency** ".
- The team regularly publishes research articles, participates in major conferences (NeurIPS, ICML, ICLR) and maintains a **dialogue** with the scientific community, regulators and the general public.
- The notion of **accountability** is also important: they believe that if an AI technology has harmful consequences, there must be **control mechanisms** and those **responsible identified** .

3.3. Collaboration and interdisciplinarity

- The founders emphasize **cooperation** with other laboratories and stakeholders, both academic and industrial.
- The subject of AI security and ethics is not just a purely technical question: Anthropic integrates profiles in

human sciences , **philosophy** , **law** or **public policy** to ensure a **global** and **multidisciplinary vision** .

3.4. Innovation oriented towards social benefit

- For Anthropic, developing more powerful models only makes sense if they serve **beneficial purposes** : improving educational tools, optimizing health services, helping with decision-making in complex environments, etc.
- This logic is in line with AI considered as a **public good** , in the same way as other major scientific advances (vaccines, fundamental discoveries).

---

4. The ethics behind Anthropic's R&D

4.1. AI Alignment as a scientific priority

- Alignment is about ensuring that language models and other AI systems behave in a way that is consistent with "positive" human intentions (avoiding inappropriate responses, not amplifying stereotypes, etc.) .
- Anthropic invests particularly in the development of **supervision mechanisms** that allow the detection and correction of undesirable behavioral deviations (hallucinations, incitement to violence, etc.).
- To do this, the company is studying approaches such as **"Constitutional AI"** , which consists of providing models with modular rules or guiding principles, inspired by ethical or legal frameworks.

4.2. Language management and moderation

- Language models like Claude, developed by Anthropic, are subject to **moderation systems** aimed at filtering inappropriate content.
- The idea is to **regulate** the learning and use of these models to limit the generation of hateful, violent, or illegal content, while respecting freedom of expression and cultural diversity.
- **detection** tools , **continuous assessment** algorithms , and dedicated policy and user support teams.

4.3. Reduce bias and promote fairness

- Like many deep learning players, Anthropic recognizes the presence of **biases** inherent in training data (gender bias, race bias, etc.).
- In its design ethos, the company emphasizes **data selection** , **bias reduction** , and **transparency** about the limitations of its models.
- The goal is to **minimize** the negative impact on minority populations and to prevent AI from perpetuating or reinforcing existing discrimination.

5. Putting it into practice: from theory to corporate culture

5.1. Internal culture and governance

- Anthropic has a **governance structure in place** to ensure that strategic decisions (which line of code to publish? which models to release?) are subject to impact analysis.
- The teams work hand in hand with external experts (academics, NGOs, regulatory bodies) to compare their choices with **ethical requirements** and **social norms** .
- Employees are encouraged to **raise** safety or liability issues if they identify them in the course of their duties.

5.2. Knowledge transfer and community engagement

- Beyond R&D, Anthropic participates in **discussion forums** , specialized **workshops , and international think tanks** on AI regulation.
- The company seeks to contribute to the training of the **next generation** of alignment researchers and experts, through the publication of articles and the encouragement of open source research (when deemed appropriate from a security perspective).

6. Conclusion: towards a resolutely responsible AI

Anthropic's **vision** , driven by its founders (Dario and Daniela Amodei, Jack Clark, etc.), is based on the idea that AI must be **designed** , **developed** , and **deployed** with a keen awareness of its short- and long-term impacts.

Their **values** and **ethics** revolve around safety , reasoned transparency , alignment , and accountability , with an approach aimed at maximizing **benefits** for society while **minimizing** risks.

By emphasizing interdisciplinarity **and** cooperation , Anthropic intends to continue its work on large language models and other AI solutions while taking into account the complexity of the real world, so that AI remains a tool at the **service** of humans and not a factor of disorder or reinforced inequalities.

The company's main projects and purpose.

1. General rationale: AI at the service of humanity, under the banner of security

1.1. The desire to avoid the excesses of AI

- Anthropic was founded to **anticipate and mitigate** the risks associated with increasingly powerful AI.
- Leaders want models, as they evolve, to remain **aligned** with human values (respect, safety, fairness, transparency) rather than serving harmful uses or even behaving unpredictably.

1.2. An "alignment" approach integrated from the design stage

- While many companies focus on model performance first, Anthropic puts **security** and **alignment** at the heart of every project.
- The idea is to create useful AIs, free (as much as possible) from bias or dangerous behavior, and capable of justifying or explaining their choices.

1.3. Focus on basic research and application

- Unlike a purely academic structure, Anthropic retains an **entrepreneurial dimension** , offering tools or services that can be used by other organizations.
- It nevertheless retains a strong **fundamental component** , because AI safety and interpretability are still areas under active exploration, requiring a lot of R&D.

2. The main projects and research areas

2.1. Claude: the great language model of Anthropic

2.1.1. Presentation of Claude

- **Claude** is one of Anthropic's flagship products, a **Large Language Model (LLM)** developed in line with Transformer-type architectures.
- It positions itself as a conversational assistant, capable of understanding user requests and providing more or less complex or nuanced responses, depending on the context.

2.1.2. Specificities of Claude

- Anthropic insisted on built-in **filtering** and **bias reduction mechanisms** from the outset, seeking to avoid the generation of violent, discriminatory, or otherwise inappropriate content.
- Claude incorporates advances from research on alignment : the use of " Constitutional **AI** " or other approaches to establish **guiding principles** on how the model should respond (e.g. ethical or legal rules).
- The model has been trained to be **cooperative** and **limit the risks of misuse** , while remaining efficient in many areas (consulting, research, writing, etc.).

2.1.3. Targeted use cases

- **Customer service** tools : automatically respond to common requests or questions.
- **Writing** assistance (texts, articles, technical documents).
- **Synthesis** and **analysis** of large volumes of textual data, to facilitate monitoring or research.
- **experimentation** to test safety and alignment mechanisms on a larger scale.

2.2. Research in AI Safety (security and alignment)

2.2.1. Studies on the "robustness" of models

- Anthropic devotes resources to assessing the extent to which large language models can be **manipulated** or incentivized to produce dangerous responses (e.g., illegal advice, hate speech).
- The idea is to design **countermeasures** (filtering, supervision, reinforcement learning, updating the "constitution" of the model) in order to **prevent** these deviations.

2.2.2. Development of evaluation protocols

- In addition to classic methods (precision tests, perplexity tests, etc.), Anthropic is experimenting with **ethical evaluation protocols** :
    - Tests in "extreme" situations, where the user deliberately tries to **push the machine** towards incorrect behavior.
    - **audit** to verify the model's compliance with the declared principles (through specialized "red teams").

2.2.3. Research on interpretability (explainability)

- Anthropic focuses on techniques for **explaining** how a language model arrived at a given answer, even though the technology of Transformers remains complex and often opaque.
- Researchers are seeking to develop tools for **neural analysis** or **visualization** of the model's internal interactions, with the aim of identifying learning patterns and possible **structural biases** .

2.3. Constitutional AI and other governance frameworks

2.3.1. Principle of constitutional AI

- The notion of " **Constitutional AI** " consists of providing the model with a **set of rules** or principles (a "constitution") that guide its behavior, for example: "respect human dignity, respect the law, prioritize truthfulness, etc."
- The goal is to **constrain** the system to follow explicit "norms," rather than relying on purely statistical optimization.

2.3.2. Collaboration with the community and regulators

- Anthropic is working with **lawyers** , **philosophers** , **NGOs** and other stakeholders to define what principles should be included in this constitution.
- The ambition is that, ultimately, these frameworks will serve as a **reference** for the entire industry, much like security **standards for electronic devices.**

2.4. Content moderation and audit tools

2.4.1. Specialized models for detecting problematic content

- Anthropic develops or uses **additional models** (classifiers) intended to automatically detect risky text categories (violence, hatred, pornography, disinformation, etc.).
- These filters can operate upstream or downstream of Claude, or other large models, and trigger **appropriate responses** (warning, refusal of treatment, etc.).

2.4.2. Independent audits and "Red Teaming"

- The company encourages **external teams** ("Red Teams") to test Claude or his search models, trying to **hijack** the system or trick it into providing harmful answers.
- The findings of these audits help improve **filters** , refine the design of AI, and share **best practices** with other organizations.

2.5. Collaboration and open research

2.5.1. Research work published in conferences

- Anthropic regularly publishes papers in renowned conferences (NeurIPS, ICML, ICLR, etc.) or on pre-print servers (arXiv), focusing particularly on the topics of **safety** , **alignment** , and **large language models** .
- This opening contributes to the **collective effort** of the AI community to better understand and master next-generation models.

2.5.2. Partnerships with other institutions

- Collaborations are established with **universities** (Stanford, Berkeley, etc.), or companies sharing similar concerns in terms of responsibility (particularly on the aspect of moderation and limits of computing power).
- The idea is to **pool** skills and spread the **culture** of AI safety and ethics to as many people as possible.

3. How these projects reflect Anthropic's purpose

3.1. Fusion between innovation and responsibility

- Anthropic isn't just developing a new chatbot or language model: it's seeking to **systematically integrate** safety, alignment, and fairness considerations into its work.
- Each project (whether Claude, Constitutional AI, moderation tools, etc.) is part of the founding **mission** : to build a beneficial, controlled AI that takes human values into account.

3.2. Concrete solutions for industry and society

- Companies or organizations that use Anthropic's services can benefit from **models already designed to protect themselves** from the risks of AI drift.
- This responds to a growing demand from customers and the public, concerned about the **responsibility** of the tools they integrate into their processes.

3.3. Influence on global AI governance

- Through its involvement in think tanks and its dialogue with **regulatory bodies** (governments, specialized commissions), Anthropic intends **to shape** the way in which civil society and decision-makers address issues of powerful AI.
- This desire to **educate** and **inspire** the community goes beyond the purely commercial field: it is an investment in the **future** of AI and its impact on humanity.

4. Conclusion

Anthropic **'s purpose** is clearly to create **safe** , **aligned** , and **transparent artificial intelligence** , prioritizing ethics **and** societal **impact** in all phases of research and development.
To achieve this vision, the company is focusing on several **key projects** :

- **Claude** , his great language model, designed from the outset to minimize the risks of malicious or biased speech.
- Extensive research on **alignment** , **robustness** and **interpretability** .
- The development of **constitutional AI** and advanced **moderation protocols** .
- Collaboration with **the** scientific community, public bodies and the private sector to share best practices and contribute to the evolution of ethical standards.

In short, Anthropic's positioning lies at the interface between cutting-edge innovation in AI and the responsibility necessary to preserve the general interest, anchoring its action in a long-term ambition: to make AI a truly **constructive tool** for society.

Chapter 3: Presentation of Claude

What is Claude?□? Its role and its main characteristics .

1. Definition and positioning of Claude

1.1. A Large Language Model (LLM) type language model

- **Claude** is a **Large Language Model** (LLM), based on technologies similar to Transformers (e.g. GPT, BERT, etc.).
- Like his counterparts, Claude is trained on **huge corpora of text** in order to learn rich **linguistic representations** and **generate** coherent and context-appropriate responses.

1.2. Created by Anthropic with safety in mind

- Claude stands out in particular by the fact that it is designed from the outset with a **focus** on **security** and **alignment** (alignment with human values).
- Anthropic, in its corporate culture, emphasizes mechanisms that **reduce** the likelihood that the model will produce inappropriate, violent, hateful, or false content.
- The name "Claude" refers to an internal project that aims for a conversational assistant that is more **reliable** and **responsible** than other general language models.

1.3. A response to the growing demand for "responsible" AI

- Several industries and companies are looking for AI systems that can interact in a **natural** and **productive way** , while avoiding ethical issues.

- Claude positions itself as a **conversational assistant** versatile enough to be integrated into various applications (customer service, content creation, analysis tools, etc.), with the advantage of more advanced **filtering** and **control** .

2. Claude's key role in the Anthropic ecosystem

2.1. A testing ground for alignment research

- Beyond simple commercial deployment, Claude serves as a **test platform** for concepts developed by the Anthropic team:
    - **AI** , where explicit ethical rules are integrated into training and inference.
    - **Moderation techniques** (automatic filters, detection of sensitive content).
    - **Audit tools** (red teams, stress test protocols).
- Feedback on Claude allows us to refine these approaches and publish research results on AI **safety** .

2.2. A conversational assistant for different sectors

- Claude can be **adapted** to various industries:
    - **Customer service** : respond to user requests, offer solutions to common problems.
    - **Writing tools** : generate texts, summaries, abstracts, etc.
    - **Research and analysis** : extract information from a large body of documents, assist analysts.
- It is therefore intended to be both a **product** for the company (generating revenue via partnerships or an API) and a **laboratory** for future technological innovations.

2.3. Emphasis on transparency and robustness

- Anthropic regularly communicates about Claude's **limitations** and the efforts undertaken to **improve** its reliability.
- The company is committed to updating the model iteratively (Claude v1, v2, etc.), taking into account feedback **from users** and the scientific community.

---

3. Main technical characteristics of Claude

3.1. Technological basis: the improved Transformer

- Like most modern LLMs, Claude is based on a **Transformer-like architecture** , introduced by the article "Attention is All You Need" (Vaswani et al., 2017).
- Anthropic has developed specific **variations** and **optimizations** , probably in the attention mechanism, the size of the network or the way of initializing the weights.
- The full details are not always entirely public, but some publications hint at **subtleties** in how Claude handles **conversational context** (memories, broader attention context, etc.).

3.2. Focus on "Constitutional AI"

- One of Anthropic's major contributions is the notion of **constitutional AI** . In concrete terms, instead of simply punishing (or "rewarding") the model as it learns through reinforcement learning, we introduce a **set of principles** (a "constitution") that the model strives to respect.
- This constitution may include **ethical rules** , **legal considerations** , or other constraints reflecting the values that Anthropic wishes to preserve.

- Claude, when providing answers, therefore takes these principles into account to **adjust** or **reframe** his generation, which differentiates him from models trained in a more "naive" manner.

3.3. Size and Datasets

- Claude is said to be comparatively **close** in size and complexity to large models like GPT-3.5 or GPT-4, although Anthropic has not always revealed an exact figure.
- The datasets include large volumes of **web texts** , but also **specialized sources** (scientific articles, legal texts, technical manuals).
- Particular care is taken in the **curation** and **filtering** of this data, to reduce the presence of toxic or poor quality content.

3.4. Filtering and moderation

- At the heart of Claude is a sophisticated **moderation module** , allowing it to **detect** and **block** (or reformulate) requests with sensitive content (explicit violence, hate speech, incitement to drugs or terrorism, etc.).
- This helps **protect** the user from unforeseen slip-ups and makes the model more suitable for enterprise use (where reputation and regulatory compliance are crucial).

3.5. Performance and benchmarks

- Although Claude is not always measured in all public **benchmarks** (e.g. MMLU, SuperGLUE, etc.), Anthropic indicates that the model **competes** with other major LLMs.
- User feedback highlights its **editorial quality** , its **ability to summarize** and its **conversational style,**

often considered more "diplomatic" or "balanced" than some competitors.

- Like any model, however, Claude can **hallucinate** (invent information), and Anthropic is working to reduce this phenomenon through internal verification techniques.

---

4. Claude Use Cases and Benefits for Users

4.1. Fluent conversational interaction

- Claude is designed to maintain a coherent **thread** , remember the context provided by the user, and **adapt** its response accordingly.
- It is particularly useful for **open-ended questions or text creation** tasks , where precision and clarity are essential.

4.2. Moderation and Compliance Assistance

- **integrated filter** mechanisms , Claude can be deployed in sensitive environments (e.g. education platform, online support).
- Organizations thus avoid resorting to external moderation solutions and benefit from a model already configured to **limit** the risks of verbal drift or illicit content.

4.3. Ethical development of AI-based products

- Companies that value AI **ethics** and responsibility **may find in Claude a partner** more aligned with these principles.
- The use of "white" AI (responsible, tested, measured) is becoming a **competitive advantage** in a market

where customers and regulators are increasingly vigilant about bias and toxic discourse.

---

5. Limitations and challenges to be addressed

5.1. Complexity of large-scale maintenance

- Like any LLM, Claude requires significant computing resources (GPU, TPU, etc.) for training **and** sometimes also for **inference** .
- **optimization** methods to offer a more profitable and accessible service, while maintaining the **power** of the model.

5.2. Persistence of bias and possibility of hallucinations

- Despite filtering efforts, it is almost impossible to eliminate **all** biases, especially those carried by training **data** .
- **erroneous** or **imprecise** answers on certain subjects, and continued fine-tuning and supervision are required.

5.3. Adaptation to regional or cultural specificities

- The ethical principles incorporated in Claude are generally formulated from a **Western (legal and cultural) point of view** .
- The company must ensure that they are **adapted** or **customized** for other contexts where **standards** and **sensitivities** may differ.

6. Conclusion

Claude is Anthropic's **great language model** , embodying the company's philosophy: putting alignment , security **and** ethics **first** .

- On the **technical level** , it is based on a Transformer-type architecture, enriched with **constitution mechanisms** (guiding rules) and advanced **moderation** .
- Functionally , Claude is suitable for a wide range of applications: customer support, writing, research, conversational assistance, with the advantage of providing more **responsible and reliable** responses than other less regulated systems.
- On the **research front** , Claude serves as a **platform** to test Anthropic's advances in AI Safety and governance, helping to shape the **practice** and **regulation** of more virtuous AI.

Ultimately, Claude illustrates Anthropic's **ambition well** : to prove that it is possible to push the limits of AI further while **reducing** the risks of abuse, in order to meet the real needs of users and society.

The technical challenges faced during its development.

1. Collection and curation of training data

1.1. The size of the corpus to be assembled

- Like any large language model, Claude requires a **considerable volume of text data** .
- These are texts from various sources: web pages, press articles, digitized works, academic documents, forums, etc.

- The **size** of the corpus can reach hundreds of gigabytes or more (often several terabytes), which involves **logistical challenges** (storage, organization, rapid access).

1.2. Filtering and data quality

- One of Anthropic's goals is to limit **bias** and **toxic content** in Claude. This requires **careful filtering** of documents:
    - Deletion or labeling of texts containing hateful, violent, or explicitly illegal language.
    - Identification of duplicate or low-quality content (spam, trivialized documents), likely to disrupt learning.
- This sorting step is particularly **delicate** : too much filtering can impoverish the diversity of the corpus, while insufficient filtering increases the risks of undesirable behavior of the model.

1.3. Linguistic and cultural heterogeneity

- Although English generally dominates in the datasets, Claude is often called upon to manage several languages or cultural registers.
- The **consistency** of the model, its respect for linguistic nuances, and the **avoidance** of erroneous generalizations constitute ongoing challenges.
- Anthropic must decide to what extent to include minority or specialist languages, while still maintaining satisfactory performance in English (or the target language).

2. Training a large-scale LLM

2.1. Hardware infrastructure: GPUs, TPUs and clusters

- Training Claude requires very high **computing resources .**
- **GPU** (NVIDIA) or **TPU (Google)** clusters to accelerate the matrix multiplication required for neural networks to operate.
- Dozens or **hundreds of** nodes can be mobilized in parallel, requiring solid **orchestration** (data distribution, gradient synchronization, failure management).
- The costs associated with electricity consumption and the rental/purchase of these resources are significant.

2.2. The complexity of the Transformer architecture

- Models based on **Transformer architecture** (self-attention mechanisms) have high algorithmic complexity, especially for long contexts (large text sequences).
- This complexity sometimes increases quadratically **with** the size of the sequence, requiring **optimizations** (sparsity, specialized kernels, etc.).
- Anthropic can use innovations such as **FlashAttention** or **Sparse Attention** to control memory consumption and reduce computation time.

2.3. Convergence problems (drive stability)

- As the **size** (number of parameters) of the model increases, the difficulties in ensuring **stable convergence** increase:
  - Risks of **vanishing** or **exploding gradients** that break learning.

- o Careful tuning of **learning rate** , **scheduler** and **hyperparameters** (batch size, normalization, etc.).
- Finding the right settings requires significant experimental **iterations** and rigorous monitoring of metrics (perplexity, cross-entropy, etc.).

2.4. Managing "catastrophic forgetting" and "continual learning"

- When new data is gradually added (for example, to update knowledge about current events), language models may forget **some** of what they have learned before.
- Anthropic must implement "continual learning" or "selective fine-tuning" **strategies** to ensure that Claude retains his past skills while integrating fresh information.
- Techniques such as **"replay mixing"** or **"long-term regularization"** can be tested.

3. The challenges of constitutional AI and alignment

3.1. Define and maintain a "constitution" of the model

- **Constitutional AI** " approach developed by Anthropic consists of integrating a **set of guiding principles** into the architecture or learning phase.
- This requires **formalizing** values such as respect, truthfulness, non-incitement to hatred, etc.
- The difficulty lies in **translating** these principles into concrete mechanisms: how should these rules be drafted? How should potentially conflicting principles

(e.g., freedom of expression vs. prevention of hate speech) be prioritized?

3.2. Human feedback reinforcement and fine-tuning

- To ensure Claude remains aligned with safe behaviors, Anthropic may use **reinforcement learning from human feedback** (RLHF) or similar approaches.
- Human evaluators assign **rewards** or **penalties** to the model's responses based on whether they meet the "constitution" or not.
- Setting up such a system is complex:
  o Annotators need **to be recruited** and **trained ,**
  o **Design** reliable labeling protocols,
  o Managing the **ambiguity** of certain topics, where the correct answer may depend on the cultural or legal context.

3.3. Reducing bias

- Even with a "constitution," Claude remains vulnerable to **biases** present in the training data.
- Anthropic must constantly **monitor** the model's responses to detect racist, sexist, or discriminatory biases.
- **Debiasing "** methods (representativeness measures, selection of alternative data, re-annotation) are essential, but they do not guarantee the total eradication of bias.

4. Real-time moderation and filtering

4.1. Automatic detection of sensitive content

- To prevent Claude from generating or relaying inappropriate content, a **moderation module** evaluates the user's prompts and/or response before restitution.
- The challenges relate to the **accuracy** of this detection: avoiding false positives (excessive censorship) and false negatives (letting harmful content through).
- Algorithms must be **constantly updated** to adapt to changes in language (new expressions, creative circumventions of prohibitions).

4.2. Managing conversational escalations

- A conversational system can be **pushed** by the user in sensitive areas: requests for illegal advice, hate speech, etc.
- Claude must be able to recognize and **refuse** or **decline** certain types of interactions, while remaining **polite** and **consistent** : it's a subtle balance.
- **Ambiguous** situations (e.g., scientific discussion on the toxicity of a substance vs. incitement to consumption) require a fine **contextual understanding** .

5. Interpretability and auditing of the model

5.1. Unraveling the Transformers "black box"

- Like other LLMs, Claude is largely a "black box": we know **how** to train it, we have its **weights** , but **understanding** the internal logic of a response remains difficult.
- Anthropic teams are seeking to develop **interpretability tools** :
  - Visualization of attention.
  - Analysis of "neural layers" to see where information is stored.

o "Feature attribution" techniques (saliency maps, etc.).

- The objectives: **detect** sources of error, **identify** potential non-compliant behavior, and **improve** user confidence.

5.2. Red teams and independent audits

- In an effort to uncover flaws or vulnerabilities, Anthropic invites " **red teams** " (external experts) to aggressively test the model.
- These experts are trying to **push** Claude to violate his constitution, to make discriminatory statements, to disclose prohibited information, etc.
- The feedback from these audits helps to **strengthen** the robustness of the system and determine future R&D projects (e.g., improving filters, rewriting constitutional principles).

---

6. Constant iteration and updating in production

6.1. Gradual deployment

- Anthropic doesn't roll out Claude to the real world all at once. The company often favors **pilot phases** or **beta tests** with select users.
- This makes it possible to identify, on a smaller scale, **borderline cases** and receive more precise **feedback** on user satisfaction.

6.2. Post-deployment maintenance and monitoring

- Once Claude is offered via an **API** or integrated into products, Anthropic must manage **updates** (new weights, fixes, adjustments to the conversational interface).

- Customer feedback (anonymized logs, problem reports) feeds into a cycle of **continuous improvement** .
- In addition, there are legal obligations (GDPR or other regulations), which sometimes impose data **traceability and the possibility of deleting** personal information.

7. Synthesis: a multidimensional challenge

The development of Claude presents Anthropic with a **series of complex technical challenges** , which lie at the intersection of **data science** , **HPC infrastructure** , **software engineering** and **responsible AI research** . These challenges can be summarized as follows:

1. **Data collection and filtering** : ensuring the quality and diversity of the corpus without letting too much problematic content through.
2. **Large-scale training** : managing computation distribution, optimizing convergence and controlling costs.
3. **Alignment approaches** : defining, formalizing and enforcing security principles, through "constitution" and learning from human feedback.
4. **Real-time moderation and filtering** : detect abuse, refuse certain requests and preserve conversational consistency.
5. **Interpretability and audit** : understand the reasons for a response, identify biases, and uncover potential flaws via red teams.
6. **Continuous iteration cycle** : progressive deployment, production maintenance, compliance with regulations and adaptation to real uses.

Each of these components raises its **share of research** and innovations, making Claude a **testing ground** where performance issues and those of **responsibility intersect** . For

Anthropic, these challenges are both obstacles to overcome and opportunities to **push the state of the art** in terms of safe and ethical AI.

Its place among other major language models (comparison with GPT, BERT, etc.).

1. Brief presentation of other major language models

1.1. GPT (Generative Pre-trained Transformer) from OpenAI

- **GPT** , available in several versions (GPT-1, GPT-2, GPT-3, GPT-4), is based on an **auto-regression** - oriented **transformer** : the model predicts the next token from the previous context.
- GPT has demonstrated the power of **self-supervised training** at scale, enabling the emergence of emergent capabilities (reasoning, zero-shot learning, text generation).
- The most recent versions, such as **GPT-4 , prove to be particularly versatile, integrating multimodality** mechanisms or relying on **alignment approaches** (reinforcement learning from human feedback, etc.).

1.2. BERT (Bidirectional Encoder Representations from Transformers) from Google

- **BERT** is a **bidirectional model** that uses masked language modeling.
- Rather than generating text, BERT focuses on language **understanding** and **analysis , proving very successful for NLP** tasks such as text classification, named entity recognition, and more.
- It marked a turning point in natural language processing (in 2018-2019) by significantly improving scores on several benchmarks.
- Unlike GPT, BERT is not designed as a large-scale generative conversational model, even though it has

inspired many variants (RoBERTa, ALBERT, DistilBERT, etc.).

1.3. Other notable models: PaLM, LLaMA, BLOOM, etc.

- **PaLM** (Google), **LLaMA** (Meta), and **BLOOM** (BigScience project) are all examples of new generation LLMs, closer to the GPT paradigm (generative, very large size).
- Some emphasize efficiency (fewer resources for inference), others openness (BLOOM is open source), or **specialization** (technical fields, regional languages).

---

2. Claude: a multi-faceted, safety-aligned LLM

2.1. Claude as a conversational model (GPT-Chat type)

- **Claude** is, like GPT (ChatGPT, GPT-4), a conversation-oriented **generative model** .
- It allows you to manage **dialogues** with users, produce coherent texts, provide explanations, and take into account chat history to respond in a contextual manner.
- In this respect, Claude is closer to a **GPT-3.5** or a **GPT-4** (whose structure is that of an auto-regressive model) rather than a purely bidirectional BERT designed for understanding.

2.2. Increased focus on alignment and security

- Claude's major specificity, compared to GPT, lies in the **level of attention** paid to **security** and **responsibility** :

- o **Constitutional AI** : Claude's designers integrate a body of principles (a "constitution") directly into the training and inference process.
  - o **filtering** : aims to refuse or redirect requests involving violence, hatred, disinformation, etc.
- GPT, on the other hand, also integrates moderation mechanisms and reinforcement learning (RLHF) to align the model, but Anthropic has made alignment **the** cornerstone of its strategy, with slightly different approaches (including the "constitutional" part).

2.3. Technical approach: "classic" transformer vs. internal innovations

- Under the hood, Claude resembles cutting-edge Transformers models (GPT-4, etc.), relying on self-**attention** and large-scale training.
- It is not (as far as is known) based on a radically different source code from the standard "Transformer", but Anthropic adds its **optimizations** and training **infrastructure (similar to OpenAI, Google Brain, etc.).**
- Full details (embedding size, number of layers, feed-forward dimension, etc.) are not always disclosed, and GPT-4 remains largely opaque.

3. Technical and philosophical points of comparison

3.1. Size and performance

- **Model size** :
  - o GPT-3.5 is approaching 175 billion parameters, GPT-4 remains unofficially encrypted (estimated at over 100 billion, potentially in the hundreds).

- BERT Large (340 million parameters) is more modest, but is an "encoder-only" model.
- Claude is probably in the **same range** as the "giant" LLMs (several tens or hundreds of billions of parameters), although Anthropic has not announced an exact number.
- **Benchmark performance** :
  - Publicly tested versions of Claude show scores **equivalent** to or sometimes higher than GPT-3.5 on certain conversational or text analysis tasks.
  - On other challenges (solving complex math problems, coding), GPT-4 might have a **slight advantage** due to its size and specific tuning.
  - Anthropic, however, publishes few comparative figures, preferring to highlight Claude's reliability and safety.

3.2. Generation style and conversational coherence

- **GPT models** are renowned for the **richness** of their responses and their ability to adapt to different registers.
- Claude, on the other hand, is characterized by a **tone that is often more diplomatic** or **balanced** , due to his filters and his "constitution". He will tend to **avoid** extremes and to think more when it comes to sensitive subjects.
- BERT is not a conversational generative model (it can be adapted to generation, but that is not its initial function), so the comparison is rather between Claude and GPT-Chat or GPT-4 on the conversational dimension.

3.3. Alignment and Refusal of Requests

- GPT and Claude share a mechanism for **detecting** inappropriate queries, but their **thresholds** and **philosophy** differ slightly.
- Claude more systematically rejects certain content, sometimes demonstrating stricter **censorship** than GPT-3.5. This is in line with Anthropic's mission to minimize the risk of abuse.
- BERT, in the context of supervised tasks, does not have a direct "conversational" component; the question of refusal or censorship arises differently (it is rather a question of filtering upstream or downstream, depending on the use).

3.4. Transparency and open source

- **GPT-4** remains very opaque about its size, structure, or precise dataset.
- **BERT** is open (official code and weights available), which has encouraged the creation of many variants.
- **Claude** , on the other hand, remains partially **the owner** : Anthropic does not publish (or not yet) the entire model, but regularly shares research elements.
- We therefore find a spectrum of confidentiality: BERT (open) <—> Claude, GPT, PaLM, etc. (closed), each organization having its reasons (cost, security, competition).

4. Differentiations in use and market positioning

4.1. Target audience and integrations

- **Claude** is offered as a **conversational service** and **API** for companies looking to incorporate an AI assistant into their products.

- GPT models (notably ChatGPT) are very widely used, accessible via a simple interface, and are also available in the form of an API (OpenAI).
- **BERT** and its derivatives are used more in the **back-end** , for specific NLP tasks (classification, QA, entity extraction) in various sectors (finance, e-commerce, healthcare, etc.).

4.2. Added value: Claude's safety as an argument

- Anthropic highlights Claude's **reliability** and **security** , assuring businesses that the model will generate less unethical or unregulated content.
- In a context where regulations and public opinion are increasingly focused on the **risks of AI** , this "responsible" positioning can give Claude a competitive advantage.
- GPT, while very popular, has a much larger user base, and OpenAI has also made significant efforts in moderation. The **differentiation** is therefore subtle and comes down to questions of **philosophy** , **priorities** , and **tolerance** for certain content.

5. Future prospects and coevolution of models

5.1. Progressive convergence of methods

- Innovations from OpenAI (such as reinforcement learning from human feedback) or Google (transformers, BERT) are influencing **the entire industry** .
- Anthropic, via Claude, brings the notion of " **Constitutional AI** " and other alignment mechanisms **that** could spread to other actors.

- As **bias** and **security issues** become more critical, we are likely to see a **convergence** of best practices (filters, red team testing, codes of conduct, etc.).

5.2. New features and multimodality

- GPT-4 introduces **multimodality** (ability to process text, images, etc.). Claude, for now, is essentially **textual** .
- It may be that in the future, Anthropic will offer a version of Claude capable of analyzing or generating images **or** videos , if this proves relevant to its mission of creating safe AI.
- The issues surrounding **security** and **filtering** of multimedia content are even more complex, which could justify a cautious roadmap.

5.3. Potential for open source or collaboration

- Like BERT (open source) and BLOOM (collaborative research model), it is possible that Anthropic will eventually release a " **light** " version of Claude for the community, or establish academic partnerships.
- These kinds of initiatives could broaden Claude's scientific impact and strengthen the **responsible AI ecosystem** .

6. Conclusion: Claude's singularity in the LLM landscape

Ultimately, **Claude** ranks among the great conversation - **oriented transformer** language **models** , playing in the same league as **GPT** (OpenAI) or **PaLM** (Google) in terms of scale and generative capabilities. However:

1. **Security philosophy** : Claude clearly stands out for the importance given to **security** and alignment **,** via his "constitution" and reinforced filtering.
2. **"Responsible" positioning** : Anthropic is banking on the fact that businesses and public authorities increasingly value **ethical compliance** , **transparency** and the **reduction of risks** linked to AI.
3. **Comparison with BERT** : Claude, like GPT, is a conversational generative model, while BERT is a bidirectional "encoder" better suited to analysis than text generation.
4. **Performance** : Feedback suggests that Claude offers a similar (or even superior in some cases) level of performance to established LLMs, while adopting a style that is often more **moderate** and **consistent** with Anthropic's ethical principles.

Thus, Claude asserts himself as a major player in the **new generation** of LLM, resolutely turned towards **responsibility and ethics** , **seeking to convince both companies and the AI community of the importance of safe** and **aligned** development .

Chapter 4: Technological Aspects of Claude

Model architecture (transformers, attention mechanisms, etc.).

1. Genesis and Basic Principles: "Attention is All You Need"

1.1. The original Transformer

- In 2017, the seminal paper **"Attention is All You Need"** (Vaswani et al.) introduced the **Transformer architecture** , revolutionizing natural language processing.
- At the heart of this model: attention (more precisely, **self-attention**), which replaces the recurrent (LSTM, GRU) or convolutional mechanisms used until now.
- Transformers are made up of stacked **blocks** (layers), each containing:
  1. A multi-headed **attention mechanism .**
  2. A feed-forward **sub-block (MLP).**
  3. **Residual connections** and normalization (LayerNorm) to stabilize and facilitate learning.

1.2. The idea of self-attention

- In a Transformer block, each **token** (word or subword) in a sentence is represented by a continuous **vector** .
- **self-attention** mechanism calculates, for each token, a weighted combination of the representations of all other tokens in the sequence.
- This allows the model to identify, at each step, the **keywords** or **grammatical dependencies** that are important for understanding the context.

- For example, in a long, complex sentence, the word "it" may refer to a subject many tokens earlier. Attention makes it easy to make these long-distance connections.

---

2. Architectural structures: encoder, decoder, or "decoder-only"

2.1. The complete encoder-decoder architecture

- In the initial diagram of "Attention is All You Need", we find an **encoder** and a **decoder** :
  - The **encoder** reads the source sequence and produces a series of internal representations.
  - The **decoder** generates a target text (e.g., for translation).
- This two-block structure is still seen in many neural translation models (e.g., Google's T5).

2.2. "Encoder-only" models (e.g. BERT)

- **BERT** relies exclusively on the "encoder" part of the Transformer.
- It is trained through "masked language modeling": some of the tokens are masked and the network learns to predict them.
- BERT excels at text **analysis** (classification, entity extraction, etc.), but is not designed to generate text autoregressively.

2.3. "decoder-only" models (e.g. GPT, Claude)

- Models such as **GPT** (and probably Claude) mainly use the **decoder part** (often in auto-regressive mode).

- This means that they generate a token-by-token sequence, where each new token is predicted based on history (the tokens already generated).
- The decoder therefore does not need a separate encoded input; the **same sequence** serves as both input and output, and the model applies "masking" ("causal" attention) so that it can only "see" past and present tokens.

For **Claude** , we can say that it follows a **decoder-only scheme** close to GPT, because it specializes in **generation** and **conversation** .

---

3. Focus on self-attention and its variants

3.1. Standard multi-head mechanism

- Each attention block is broken down into several "heads." Each head learns to identify different **types of relationships** between tokens (e.g., syntactic, semantic, positional, etc.).
- The heads are then **concatenated** and passed through a linear projection, before passing to the feed-forward part.
- This multi-head arrangement allows for fine modeling of several aspects of the context in parallel.

3.2. Causal attention for generation

- In an **autoregressive model , a " mask "** is applied so that each token can only pay attention to previous tokens (and itself), never to future tokens.
- **bidirectional** attention , where each token can consider the entire sequence (past/future).

- Claude, being conversational and generative, therefore incorporates this causal attention, allowing him to "predict" the next token step by step, like GPT.

3.3. Recent Attention Optimizations

- At large scales, attention can become **expensive** (quadratic complexity as a function of sequence length). **Sparse attention** or **sliding window techniques** are sometimes employed.
- Researchers also propose mechanisms like **FlashAttention** , **Longformer** , **Big Bird** , etc., to handle larger pop-ups at lower cost.
- Anthropic hasn't revealed for sure what precise optimizations Claude implements, but it's likely to contain **adaptations** that extend the useful context while controlling the computational load.

---

4. Feed-forward blocks (MLP) and residual connections

4.1. Feed-forward sub-block (position-wise FFN)

- After each attention module, there is a **feed-forward neural network** (often called "FFN" or "MLP block").
- It acts independently **on** each token, transforming the vector representation resulting from attention.
- Typically, we have a higher-dimensional linear layer, an activation (e.g., GeLU), then a projection to the original dimension.
- This step helps increase **the** "representational capacity" of the model, which is crucial for capturing complex regularities in language.

4.2. Residual connections and normalizations

- Within a block, we often apply a **residual connection** around attention and feed-forward, as well as a **Layer Normalization** (LayerNorm) before or after these sub-blocks.
- Residual connections (invented in ResNet) help improve **gradient** propagation and avoid "vanishing gradient".
- LayerNorm stabilizes the distribution of activations, making learning more robust, especially for large networks .

---

5. Embeddings and positioning in the sequence

5.1. Word embeddings vs. token embeddings

- The models handle **tokenization** (often with BPE or SentencePiece), slicing the text into subunits. Each token receives an **embedding vector** .
- These embeddings are learned during the pre-training phase, and constitute the **initial representation** of each token before entering the Transformers blocks.

5.2. Positional embeddings

- To make a Transformer "know" where a token is located in the sequence, we add **position information to it** .
- The original paper uses **sinusoids** (Positional Encoding). Other approaches (Rotary Embeddings, ALiBi, etc.) offer more flexible ways to incorporate the notion of position.
- Positional integration often determines the model's **ability** to handle long contexts: if the positioning method does not scale well, the model may degrade its performance over very long sequences.

5.3. Expanding the pop-up window

- Recent LLMs (GPT-4, Claude, etc.) tend to increase the **context window** beyond the "classic" 2,048 tokens (GPT-3).
- Claude, for example, could support several thousand tokens, allowing for long **conversations** or more in-depth contextual analyses.
- Infrastructure upgrades (more memory, better attention algorithms) are required to scale up.

---

6. Self-supervised training and alignment strategies

6.1. Self-supervised pre-training phase

- Like GPT, Claude follows a massive **pre-training phase** on a large corpus of unannotated texts, predicting the next token (auto-regression).
- Over **thousands** or **millions** of iterations, the model learns the language structure, semantics, etc.
- This expensive step requires huge **GPU/TPU resources** , distribution **across** multiple nodes, and continuous monitoring of **metrics** (loss, perplexity).

6.2. Fine-tuning and RLHF

- After this pre-training, Claude is refined via specific **fine-tuning** :
  - **RLHF (Reinforcement Learning from Human Feedback)** , where human annotators evaluate the generated responses, indicating whether they are satisfactory or not.
  - **Constitutional AI** : Incorporating a "set of rules" or "guiding principles" into learning,

aimed at reducing harmful or unethical
responses.
- These steps transform a purely statistical model into a
conversational assistant aligned with security and
courtesy.

7. Possible peculiarities in Claude

7.1. Rumors and clues

- Anthropic has not released the full **source code** or
complete architectural diagram of Claude, but it can be
surmised that:
    o Claude adopts a **"decoder-only" structure**
    close to GPT.
    o **pop-up window** handling to allow for longer
    and more complex conversations.
    o **Attention modifications** , like FlashAttention
    or others, could be present to better scale on
    large volumes of tokens.
    o Training uses stricter data filtering **protocols**
    (to avoid toxicity, illegal content), and
    extensive hyperparameter tuning to stabilize
    convergence .

7.2. Emphasis on robustness and built-in moderation

- The architecture is accompanied by an **upstream** and
downstream moderation **pipeline** :
    o Detect "sensitive" prompts and prevent the
    model from producing non-character content.
    o Post-process the generation to filter out certain
    violent/angry words or suggestions.
- This **layer** is not just a modification of the network, but
a set of **policies** and **modules** connecting Claude to the
constitution of Anthropic (these aspects, although

extra-architectural, influence the way the model is exploited).

---

8. Conclusion: A new generation Transformer designed for conversation

Ultimately, **Claude** inherits the **fundamental skeleton** of the Transformers:

1. **blocks containing a causal multi-head attention** module , followed by a **feed-forward sub-block** and punctuated by **residual connections** and **LayerNorm** .
2. Embeddings of tokens and positions (with a technical **solution** adapted to manage long contexts).
3. **Preliminary** self-supervised training on a large text corpus, before fine - **tuning** geared towards conversation and security (RLHF, Constitutional AI).

What sets Claude apart is its emphasis on **safety** , **alignment** , and the desire to include, from the design stage, a **"constitution"** that regulates its responses and behavior. In terms of **internal architecture** , it remains very close to "decoder-only" GPT models—a consistent choice for a large-scale generative **conversational assistant** .

innovation is therefore not only in the "form" of the Transformer (which they refine according to the best practices of the AI community), but in the **purpose and** philosophy **surrounding** its use: to give birth to a **powerful AND responsible LLM** , capable of supporting long discussions in a safe manner and aligned with predefined ethical principles.

Training and datasets used.

1. The foundations of training: large-scale self-supervision

1.1. Principle of self-supervision

- Like most LLMs (GPT, PaLM, LLaMA, etc.), Claude is **pre-trained** in **self-supervised mode** :
    - The model is presented with **texts** (divided into tokens) and it learns to predict the next token, without needing classic human labels.
    - This method exploits very large volumes of textual data, making it possible to learn the syntactic, semantic and contextual regularities of the language.

1.2. Objectives and scale

- The ambition is to cover a **wide spectrum** of subjects, registers (formal, familiar), styles (article, dialogue, code, etc.), so that Claude can be **versatile** .
- Contemporary models (Claude, GPT-3.5, GPT-4) can train on corpora ranging from **hundreds of gigabytes** to several **terabytes** of text, gathered from various sources (web, literature, code, etc.).

---

2. The main sources of textual data

2.1. Common Crawl, Wikipedia and other public databases

- **Common Crawl** : Often at the heart of web datasets, it is a vast "raw" corpus exploring trillions of words from different web pages.
- **Wikipedia** : an essential source for more qualitative content, covering a wide range of fields (science, history, culture, etc.).
- **Code repositories** : Some LLMs include files from development platforms (GitHub, etc.) to help you master code generation and comprehension. It's plausible that Anthropic integrates some of these to broaden Claude's skills, although this isn't systematically confirmed.

2.2. Books, articles and specialized archives

- Many research laboratories (including Anthropic) supplement their corpus with **book archives** (projects such as BooksCorpus, or even internal collections).
- **Press articles** and **academic publications** : content relevant to understanding more complex or expert texts (science, technology, human sciences).
- The goal is to obtain a rich palette:
    - o Factual texts,
    - o Literature,
    - o Journalistic content,
    - o Technical texts...

2.3. Filtered and verified data

- A crucial part of the job is **filtering** these sources: eliminating spam, duplicates, low-quality texts, pornographic or violent content, etc.
- Because Anthropic has a strong **commitment to safety** , it is likely that they conduct even **more extensive screening** than other labs to reduce the presence of problematic content.

- The idea is not to eliminate all types of speech, but to remove anything that might **interfere** with learning or push the model toward harmful behaviors.

---

3. Curation and bias reduction strategies

3.1. Selection and qualitative classification

- **classification** steps :
  - Detect and remove "toxic" texts (hate speech, threats, etc.) in large or partial quantities,
  - Identify specific **languages** or **dialects** ,
  - Check the "density" or "coherence" of a document (deletion of documents that are too noisy, without understandable sentences).

3.2. Socio-cultural biases and diversity

- Even with filtering, the **issue of bias** remains: if the corpus leans too much towards one culture or point of view (e.g., English-speaking and Western), the model risks reproducing certain stereotypes.
- We know that Anthropic initiatives aim to expand the spectrum of data (texts from minorities, from less represented regions of the globe, etc.).
- However, the balance between **diversity** and **quality** remains delicate: too much filtering can suppress legitimate communities or registers, while overrepresentation of one culture imposes other biases.

3.3. Partial transparency

- Anthropic, like OpenAI or Google, does not always publicly reveal the **exhaustive list** of included sites or all the filtering criteria, partly to protect proprietary aspects or to prevent some from "circumventing" the filters.

- **deduplication** techniques , keyword **moderation , and internal classifier models** to identify non-compliant content.

---

4. Training organization: phases and infrastructure

4.1. Massive pre-workout (stage 1)

- As mentioned, Claude goes through a self-supervised pre-training phase, where he "absorbs" gigantic amounts of text.
- This process takes place on GPU/TPU **clusters** (probably several hundred processors in parallel).
- **gradient descent** methods (Adam, Lamb, etc.) and requires distributed coordination (e.g., Microsoft DeepSpeed's **ZeRO , or Megatron-LM**).
- Monitored metrics include **loss** (often cross-entropy) and **perplexity** (the model's ability to guess the correct token).

4.2. Fine-tuning and alignment (stage 2)

- Once the model has acquired the basics of language, Anthropic moves on to **alignment steps** to make it safer and more "conversational".
- This phase combines:
    - o RLHF **(** Reinforcement Learning from Human Feedback), where generated text samples are annotated by humans, indicating whether the response is adequate, harmful or inaccurate.
    - o **Constitutional AI "** approach , where a set of **principles** (ethical rules, moderation guidelines) is injected into the learning process.

- At this point, Anthropic may add a **dataset** specifically designed for instruction (question/answer pairs, dialogues) or **safety** (examples of abuse, offensive language, etc., with the "correct" moderation response).

4.3. Testing, Iterations and Deployment

- The team then tests Claude in **real** or simulated conditions (red team, stress tests), to track:
    - The persistence of **bias** or dangerous responses,
    - Hallucinations (factual inventions) ,
    - Behaviors contrary to the "constitution" of the model.
- At the end of this phase, we decide whether the model is ready to be **deployed** (in the form of an API, for example) or whether it requires a new fine-tuning session.
- This loop of **iterations** can continue indefinitely, with successive "versions" (Claude v1, v1.2, v2, etc.).

5. Probable composition of the "training mix" for Claude

Although we do not have a precise list of Anthropic's datasets, we can make some realistic **estimates** based on practices in the field:

1. **Corpora Web** (Common Crawl, WebText-like, filtered):
    - Represents a large part of the volume (often more than 50%).
    - Gives the model its linguistic **versatility** and knowledge of the "real world".
2. **Wikipedia** (all relevant languages):
    - A qualitative core for general knowledge, structured and often reliable.

       o Can represent 1 to 5% of the total, but a significant percentage for quality.

3. **Books corpus** :
       o Several gigabytes, including classic literature, novels, essays, etc.
       o Brings a more fluid **writing style** and narrative **coherence** .

4. **Conversational data** (forums, various dialogues, anonymized chat logs):
       o Important for the **conversational assistant dimension** .
       o May include filtered Reddit, other community platforms, etc.
       o Essential for learning **"turn taking"** , the **context** in an exchange, etc.

5. **Specialized data** (technical documentation, research articles, code, etc.):
       o To give the model **competence** on more advanced subjects (math, science, programming).
       o Their share can be moderate (a few percent), but targeted in order to enrich the capacity for reasoning or problem-solving.

6. **Internal data at the fine-tuning stage** :
       o Anthropic-annotated question-answer pairs, practice dialogues, examples of "delicate" prompts (sensitive content) to refine **moderation** and **alignment** .
       o This is a much lower volume than pre-workout, but it has a **considerable impact** on Claude's final behavior.

---

6. The challenges and difficulties of large-scale training

6.1. Cost and logistics

- Training an LLM of Claude's caliber involves **very high costs** (machine time, cooling, electricity, specialized engineers).
- Companies like Anthropic often invest tens **of millions of dollars** to make a single large training cycle possible.
- Infrastructures must be robust to handle model **distribution** across hundreds of GPUs/TPUs in parallel.

6.2. Quality and bias monitoring

- Despite careful filtering, there is a constant **risk of certain stereotypes** or **hate speech** resurfacing .
- Teams must check the balance of the data, identify potential " **hot spots** " of misinformation and iterate to improve the corpus.

6.3. Continuous update

- The world is changing, new information is emerging (current events, new laws, scientific discoveries).
- Anthropique must schedule regular **fine** -tuning or re-training to keep Claude up to date and prevent him from "stagnating" in an outdated vision.
- **Continual learning** " or " **partial retraining** " techniques are being explored to minimize "catastrophic forgetting" (the risk of losing old skills when integrating new data).

---

7. Conclusion: a massive and evolving mix

In summary, Claude's **training** is based on:

- **Huge text corpora** from the web (Common Crawl, Wikipedia, books, etc.), carefully **filtered** and **selected** to avoid toxicity or digital waste.
- A **learning process** in two major stages: **self-supervised pre-training** (to acquire the linguistic and factual basis) then **fine-tuning** (to make it aligned, safe and conversational, thanks to "Constitutional AI" and RLHF).
- A **continuous cycle of validation** and update, which involves "red teams" and audit protocols to detect deviations in behavior and adjust filters or "constitution."

In this sense, Claude does not fundamentally differ from large language models such as GPT, PaLM or LLaMA in terms of pre-training (since they all use similar approaches). However, Anthropic stands out for its even greater **commitment** to **safety** , ethics **and** data curation, in order to minimize the risks of harmful or biased speech. The result is reflected in the **conversational quality** and final **alignment** of Claude, which is an integral part of the company's "raison d'être".

Specific optimizations (learning rates, natural language processing, etc.).

1. Optimizations related to learning rates

1.1. The learning rate and its variations

- The choice of a **learning rate** is crucial for the **stability** and **speed** of convergence.
- For large language models (LLMs), a relatively low initial **learning rate** or "warm-up" scheme is often used, and then this rate is gradually **reduced** according to a predefined plan.

1.1.1. The warm-up

- In the early stages of training, the learning rate is gradually increased over a number of iterations (e.g., over 1% to 5% of the total training).
- This avoids divergence problems when the weights are random and the gradient can explode.
- After this phase, we adopt a **plateau** or we begin a **decrease** in the learning rate.

1.1.2. Decline patterns

- The most common include **linear decay** or **cosine annealing** (where the learning rate follows an inverse cosine curve).
- Other adaptive approaches (e.g. **Adam** , **AdamW** , **LAMB**) automatically handle the evolution of the internal rate for each parameter, optimizing convergence on gigantic models.

1.2. "Large Batch Training"

- With a large number of **GPUs** in parallel, we can increase the **batch size** (number of examples per iteration).
- Large **Batch Training** allows for more parallel computation, but can degrade generalization if the learning rate and hyperparameters are not tuned correctly.
- Techniques like **LAMB** (Layer-wise Adaptive Moments for Batch Training) help maintain stability for massive batches by adjusting gradients appropriately for each layer.

1.3. Gradient accumulation

- When **GPU memory** is limited or a larger "effective batch" is desired, **gradient accumulation is used** .
- This involves **accumulating** gradients over multiple mini-batches before performing the final backpropagation.
- This results in a larger effective batch, without exploding the GPU RAM, at a cost in **number of iterations** .

---

2. Distributed processing and parallelism optimizations

2.1. Data Parallelism

- The simplest method: divide the entire data set (batches) between several **GPUs/nodes** .
- Each GPU calculates the **loss** and **gradients** on its portion, then the gradients are **averaged** to update the weights synchronously (Distributed Data Parallel).
- Frameworks like **PyTorch DDP** , **Horovod** or **DeepSpeed** make these operations easier.

2.2. Model Parallelism

- When a model reaches **hundreds** of billions of parameters, a single GPU can no longer store all the weights.
- The model is then divided into **blocks** (pipeline parallelism) or **tensors** (tensor parallelism) to distribute the loads between several GPUs.
- **Megatron-LM** (NVIDIA) and **DeepSpeed** (Microsoft) implement these approaches in advanced ways, sometimes combining data parallelism and model parallelism for massive scale.

2.3. Hybrid optimizations (ZeRO, etc.)

- **ZeRO** (Zero Redundancy Optimizer) reduces redundancy in storing gradients, parameters, and optimizer states, distributed across different nodes.
- This helps **reduce** the memory consumed on each GPU, train larger models, and speed up communication between nodes.

2.4. Gradient checkpointing

- A technique to **save** memory during iteration: instead of keeping all intermediate activations for backpropagation, only certain "checkpoints" are retained.
- During backpropagation, missing activations are **recalculated** . This increases computation time, but **reduces memory consumption** .

---

3. Optimizations for language processing (tokenization, text pipeline)

3.1. Subword Tokenization

- Large models almost all employ **sub-word tokenization** (BPE, SentencePiece, WordPiece, etc.) to handle vocabulary **variability and the presence of rare or unseen words.**
- Thus, an unknown term is split into subunits, avoiding introducing "unknown" tokens (OOV).
- This approach ensures a more compact **vocabulary** (in the order of 30,000 to 100,000 tokens) and covers a wide range of languages.

3.2. Text cleaning and standardization

- Before tokenization, standardization is often carried out (removal of unwanted characters, unicodification, etc.).
- For certain complex or ideogrammic languages (Chinese, Japanese), a specific preprocess may be necessary (segmentation into characters or sub-characters).

3.3. Management of sensitive content

- Anthropic (via Claude) highlights the importance of **filtering** or classifying **the** text upstream:
  - Identify violent, hateful, etc. passages.
  - Apply strategies (deletion, masking, annotation) to better control learning.
- Optimization is therefore also at the level of the data preparation **pipeline , not only in the hyperparameters of the architecture.**

---

4. Optimized accuracy and reduced GPU consumption

4.1. Mixed training: FP16/BF16

- Using **half-precision** (Float16, bfloat16) has become the standard to speed up matrix computing on GPUs and save memory.
- Modern cards (NVIDIA Ampere, Google TPU) natively manage **Mixed Precision** (internal calculation in FP16/BF16, accumulation in FP32 for stability).
- This can increase training **speed by 2-3 times or more depending on the configuration.**

4.2. Gradient control (clipping)

- Gradient **clipping** (by L2 norm, for example) prevents overly abrupt updates and stabilizes convergence.
- Combined with mixed optimization (FP16), this also limits the risks of **overflow** (infinite values).

4.3. Quantization techniques for inference

- Although not always used during training, **quantization methods** (8 bits, 4 bits) can be applied in the inference phase to reduce the model size and speed up the response, sometimes without degrading the quality too much.
- We can imagine that Anthropic is working on these solutions to deploy lighter versions of Claude, or to integrate it into more restricted devices.

5. Advanced approaches for coherent and controlled generation

5.1. "Constitutional AI" and inference rules

- Beyond learning algorithms, inference (or generation) benefits from specific mechanisms to **restrict** or **correct** responses.

- Techniques such as **rewriting** (post-processing), adding "fix" **prompts** , or injecting manual **rules** can be used to keep the model within a "secure" framework.

5.2. Decoding algorithms (top-k, nucleus sampling, etc.)

- Classical approaches for inference include **greedy search** , **beam search** , **top-k sampling** , **nucleus sampling** (top-p).
- **Top-k** : The model selects from the k most likely tokens at each step, which can increase **diversity** compared to purely deterministic selection.
- **Nucleus (top-p)** : we sample from the smallest set of tokens whose sum of probabilities reaches p (e.g. 0.9).
- The choice of decoding algorithm influences the style, creativity, and **consistency** of the response.

5.3. Style and Tone Control

- Some labs are experimenting with **"prefix tokens"** or "control codes" to guide style (more formal, more concise, etc.).
- At Anthropic, we can imagine a dimension of optimization where Claude integrates **"preferences"** or ethical instructions, modifying the style of his responses in the direction of politeness, moderation, etc.

---

6. Monitoring metrics and experimental settings

6.1. Perplexity and cross-entropy

- During training, **perplexity** or **cross-entropy** remain key indicators of the model's ability to predict tokens.

- Too high or stagnant perplexity indicates that hyperparameters (learning rate, batch size, etc.) need to **be adjusted .**

6.2. Internal and external benchmarks

- Beyond perplexity, **validation sets are used** to assess **answer quality , security** (e.g., drift tests, sensitive questions), and **reasoning ability** on public datasets (SQuAD, MMLU, Big-Bench, etc.).
- Anthropic may have **internal benchmarks** dedicated to evaluating "Constitutional AI": toxicity tests, red team prompts, etc.

6.3. Failure management and retraining

- Training a model at this scale often results in " **winters** " where the model diverges or performs poorly.
- The engineers then return to the configuration (cadences, architecture, distribution) to understand the cause: a **learning rate** that is too high, a batch size problem, a bug in the parallel code, etc.

---

7. Conclusion: a coordinated set of techniques

Ultimately, the **specific optimizations** for training a large language model like Claude are not limited to simply adjusting the **learning rate** . They form a complete **ecosystem** :

1. **Fine-grained planning** of the learning rate (warm-up, decay, adaptive optimizers).
2. **Parallelism techniques** (data parallel, model parallel, ZeRO) to manage the astronomical number of parameters and ensure good **scalability** .

3. **Intelligent precision management** (FP16, BF16, gradient clipping) to reconcile **speed** , **memory** and **stability** .
4. Text **tokenization** and **preprocessing pipeline, including filtering and classification, ensuring** corpus **quality** and **security** .
5. **Control of inference** and generation , via sampling algorithms and "Constitutional AI" rules, ensuring behavioral and ethical alignment.
6. **Monitoring** metrics and constant adjustments to optimize the **quality** and **robustness** of the model over iterations.

This orchestration of multiple technical elements is found in all leading AI labs, and Anthropic is working to push these methods even further, given its particular focus on security **and** alignment . The result is a **large operational language model** , capable of powerful conversational interactions while **minimizing** the risk of drift or major errors.

Management of bias and ethical issues integrated into the development process.

1. Understanding the origin of bias in LLMs

1.1. Biases inherited from the data corpus

- **Language models** like Claude learn from large volumes of text collected from the internet, books, code repositories, etc.
- These data are **loaded** with cultural, historical, sociological representations: certain groups are over- or under-represented, certain worldviews dominate, etc.
- For example, if the corpus contains a significant proportion of texts presenting gender stereotypes, the model risks **reproducing** these stereotypes.

1.2. Biases amplified by self-learning

- Self **-supervision** (predicting the next token on massive corpora) does not intrinsically differentiate between stereotype-laden text and nuanced text, because there is no explicit "ethical label."
- Models sometimes "amplify" encountered statistical regularities, including harmful biases.
- If a minority demographic group appears less often or less positively in the data, the model may develop incorrect or discriminatory **associations** .

1.3. Structural biases linked to algorithms

- **induced** " biases :
  - Tokenization decisions (some non-Western language words are incorrectly segmented).
  - Training decisions (how do we handle incomplete sentences, time series, etc.?).

- Although these "algorithmic" biases are less obvious than cultural biases, they can influence the distribution of responses (e.g., unequal treatment of a dialect or writing system).

---

2. Strategies for detecting and mitigating bias

2.1. Upstream data filtering and curation

- Even before training, Anthropic (like other laboratories) carries out a **sorting** to eliminate:
    - Content that is clearly hateful, discriminatory, or violent.
    - Dubious sources (spam, massive fake news).
- They use **classification models** or keyword lists, as well as more advanced heuristics (hate speech detection).
- This filtering reduces the proportion of toxic texts, but it does not eliminate more subtle biases (implicit stereotypes).

2.2. Statistical approaches to bias detection

- Once a model is pre-trained, we can design tests **to** spot unfair trends:
    - Evaluate the distribution of responses for various demographic groups (e.g., a prompt "The doctor is...", "The leader is...", "The housewife is...").
    - Measure **polarity scores** or implicit association rates (related to research on the IAT – Implicit Association Test).
- The results guide the implementation of **countermeasures** during fine-tuning, by correcting or rebalancing examples where the model displays a strong bias.

2.3. Fine-tuning and reinforcement learning (RLHF)

- Anthropic applies **"Constitutional AI"** and **RLHF** (Reinforcement Learning from Human Feedback) to define **rules** limiting the production of biased or offensive responses.
- Human annotators evaluate the model's responses on sensitive items (e.g., questions related to gender, race, religion) and assign feedback (positive, negative).
- The model thus learns to **avoid** pejorative formulations, stereotypes or any potentially discriminatory content.
- However, this is a **complex process** : an "excess" of censorship could also mask realities or hinder legitimate freedom of expression.

2.4. Debiasing by reweighting or recalibration

- Some labs are testing more targeted **"debiasing" techniques** :
  - **Reweighting** samples (increasing the weight of texts that counteract dominant biases).
  - **Counterfactual data augmentation** : generating sentence variants where certain attributes (gender, ethnicity) are swapped, in order to push the model to treat these attributes fairly.
- These methods can be used in addition to high-level fine-tuning, in order to better manage the **blind spots** identified by the ethics team.

---

3. Ethical issues in the development process

3.1. Representation and cultural plurality

- A model like Claude is intended for international use, in diverse contexts. However, conceptions of what constitutes "acceptable speech" vary greatly between regions, cultures, and legislation.

- Defining a " **universal charter** " of moderation is becoming difficult. Anthropic proposes its "constitution," but how can we ensure that it respects the **diversity** of cultural or religious sensitivities?
- Ethical arbitration is therefore a **permanent project** : too much laxity risks tolerating excesses, too much censorship can stifle freedom of expression.

3.2. Transparency and explainability

- Laboratories are often criticized for a **lack of clarity** about data provenance and moderation principles.
- From an ethical point of view, it is desirable that users and researchers know **how** a model was filtered, trained, and what values drive its responses (anthropique publishes or partially explains the broad outlines of its "Constitutional AI").
- However, too much transparency can allow malicious actors to find **flaws** (circumvention of filters, malicious exploitation).

3.3. Responsibility and accountability

- Who is **responsible** if Claude produces sexist, racist or violence-inciting responses?
- Legally, AI regulations (e.g. the European AI Act) could require designers to implement a system for **monitoring** and **traceability** of algorithmic decisions.
- Public trust is also at stake. Anthropic aims to be at the forefront of these issues, but adapting to different legal contexts (United States, EU, etc.) is a constant challenge.

3.4. Surveillance and Big Brother

- A reverse risk is that the company, to reduce bias, deploys **monitoring mechanisms** that are too invasive in the data or in the use of the model.
- Ethics dictates finding the **right balance** : moderating and correcting without infringing too much on the privacy of contributors or the neutrality of access to information.
- Anthropic's internal policy usually includes **guidelines** regarding log collection and storage, anonymization, etc.

---

4. Alignment and "Constitutional AI": a framework to reduce bias

4.1. Principle of the "Constitution"

- In Claude's case, Anthropic introduces a "set of rules" (a form of "constitution") that the model must **respect** during inference and fine-tuning.
- There you will find:
    1. Principles of **non-discrimination** (not spreading hateful content towards a group).
    2. **Limitation** rules (violent, explicit, illegal content).
    3. Injunctions to be **courteous** and precise (avoid misinformation).

4.2. Practical application

- Technically, this involves:
    - prompts or **scripts** inserted into the template (e.g. "You must politely decline when asked…", "You respond impartially about group X…").
    - Reinforced learning (RLHF) where annotators report if the answer violates the constitution.

- Thus, the **detection** of bias, the **neutralization** of certain drifts and the **preservation** of a "respectful" tone become explicit objectives of the model.

4.3. Limitations and criticisms

- Every constitution reflects a **value system** (Western, in most cases). Some will argue that local adjustments are necessary depending on culture or legislation.
- Too many rules can lead the model to censor themselves excessively or refuse to discuss legitimate topics (e.g., politics, religion, etc.).
- Anthropic and the AI community continue to seek solutions to enable model **customization** while avoiding misuse (e.g., "If I allow the user to release filters, could I facilitate hate speech?").

---

5. Continuous monitoring and improvement process

5.1. Red teams and independent audits

- The **red teams** (internal or external) test the model by deliberately trying to **push** Claude to produce content that is illicit, discriminatory, or contrary to the stated ethical principles.
- Their feedback is used to **iterate** : correct the rules, adjust the model, improve the content classifier.
- This audit loop is essential because malicious (or simply curious) users are always discovering new vulnerabilities.

5.2. Updating the corpus and fine-tuning

- Societal biases are evolving, new forms of extremist expression are appearing, new dialects are…

- Anthropic must regularly **refresh** its dataset and update moderation rules to keep pace with cultural, political, and legal developments.
- **alignment** process is never "finished"; it is an **accompaniment** of the model throughout its life cycle.

5.3. Collaboration with the AI community

- To address these complex issues, many labs and researchers advocate **transparency** , the **sharing** of bias detection tools, and the **publication** of studies on the assessment of toxicity or discrimination.
- Anthropic participates in conferences and working groups on **AI security** , aiming to standardize practices (drafting standards, white papers, etc.).

6. Conclusion: continued vigilance for more ethical AI

The management of biases and ethical issues integrated into Claude's development results in:

1. **filtering** and **curation** of the corpus to reduce the initial intake of toxic content.
2. **evaluation and correction mechanisms** (fine-tuning, RLHF, Constitutional AI), actively targeting discriminatory or violent behavior.
3. The **establishment** of guiding principles (the "constitution") and an internal culture of **ethics** , which goes beyond strict technical parameters.
4. auditing (red teams, stress tests) and **continuous improvement** through feedback from the public and experts, with a view to responsibility towards society.

Despite these efforts, "zero risk" does not exist. AI's biases and ethical issues reflect—and sometimes amplify—those of society. The role of Anthropic, and of all stakeholders in the field, is therefore to **minimize** these biases as much as possible, **maintain** relative transparency about the choices made, and **continue** to refine the model as new challenges emerge.

Chapter 5: Claude's Use Cases

Examples of applications in different sectors (customer service, writing, education, etc.).

1. Customer Service

1.1. Automated assistance and chatbots

- **Instant answers:**
  Claude can be integrated into chatbot systems to answer frequently asked customer questions 24/7, reducing wait times and call center costs. For example, in an airline, the model can provide information on flight schedules, baggage policies, or booking procedures.
- **Managing complex requests:**
  Thanks to his ability to understand the context of a conversation, Claude can handle more complex requests that require a detailed understanding of the situation. For example, in a banking department, he might guide a customer through a technical issue or explain security procedures.

1.2. Personalization of the customer experience

- **Preference analysis:**
  By processing large volumes of customer data, Claude can help personalize interactions. For example, it can tailor responses based on the user's profile, recommend products, or anticipate needs, creating a more seamless and engaging customer experience.
- **Feedback and continuous improvement:**
  The interactions generated by Claude can be analyzed to extract satisfaction indicators, allowing companies to

better understand their customers' expectations and adjust their services accordingly.

---

2. Writing and content creation

2.1. Text generation and assisted writing

- **Articles and Blogs:**
  Claude can generate blog posts, press releases, or marketing content with a specific tone and style. Writers can use this as a starting point to speed up content production, while manually refining the text for greater precision or creativity.
- **Creative Content Creation:**
  In literature or advertising, Claude can propose narrative ideas, generate slogans or even write short scripts, thus offering creators a tool for brainstorming and rapid prototyping.

2.2. Synthesis and rewriting tools

- **Automatic Summarization:**
  For long documents or technical reports, Claude can summarize information into a few clear sentences, thus assisting in decision-making or the dissemination of essential information in professional or educational contexts.
- **Rewriting and paraphrasing:**
  The template can be used to reword texts, correct inconsistencies or adapt content for a specific audience, thus ensuring greater clarity and stylistic consistency.

---

3. Education and training

3.1. Personalized educational assistance

- **Virtual Tutors:**
  Claude can act as an online tutor, answering students' questions on a variety of topics, from mathematics to literature. His ability to explain concepts in an accessible manner complements traditional teaching, particularly for distance learning.
- **Educational Content Creation:**
  Teachers can use Claude to generate course materials, interactive quizzes, and lesson summaries, facilitating educational preparation and real-time program updates.

3.2. Revisions and self-study aids

- **Dialogue simulations:**
  For foreign language or communication courses, Claude can simulate realistic conversations, allowing learners to practice in a virtual environment without the pressure of a human interlocutor.
- **Explanation of complex concepts:**
  In science or philosophy, the model can provide detailed explanations adapted to the student's level of understanding, thus promoting better assimilation of knowledge.

---

4. Health and well-being

4.1. Medical information and online assistance

- **Patient Support:**
  In the medical field, Claude can provide information on symptoms, explain procedures or give general health

advice (always specifying that he is not a substitute for professional medical advice).
- **Document research assistance:**
Healthcare professionals can use the template to synthesize scientific research, update their knowledge on the latest medical advances, or prepare clinical reports.

4.2. Psychological assistance

- **Supportive chatbots:**
While requiring special vigilance to avoid crossing the boundaries of medical practice, Claude can serve as a psychological support tool by offering empathetic responses and directing users to resources or qualified professionals when needed.

---

5. Finance and Business

5.1. Financial data analysis

- **Report Writing:**
In the financial sector, Claude can help generate market reports, analyze economic trends or synthesize information from multiple sources to provide strategic analyses to decision-makers.
- **Compliance Automation:**
The template can be used to check document compliance or to draft complex regulatory summaries, making the work of legal and compliance departments easier.

5.2. Customer Relationship Management (CRM) Support

- **Communication Management:**
  For sales and support teams, Claude can automate email writing, customer request responses, and relationship management via CRM platforms, improving the efficiency of sales interactions.

6. Media and Entertainment

6.1. Generation of scenarios and interactive content

- **Narrative Game Creation:**
  In the video game industry, Claude can be used to generate interactive dialogues or complex scenarios, enriching the narrative experience of video games or interactive applications.
- **Media Personalization:**
  Streaming platforms and content producers can use the model to adapt scripts, generate series summaries, or even create original content in collaboration with writers.

6.2. Assistance to journalists

- **Writing and Verification:**
  For newsrooms, Claude can help write summary articles, quickly check facts, or reword information to fit different media formats.
- **Sentiment analysis:**
  The model can analyze data streams (social media, online comments) to assess public sentiment on a topic, helping journalists understand and contextualize the news.

7. Other cross-cutting applications

7.1. Research and development support

- **Synthesis of scientific documents:**
  Researchers can use Claude to extract key points from academic publications, generate bibliographies or even formulate research hypotheses.
- **Project management:**
  In the world of innovation, the model can help structure projects, write grant proposals, or synthesize feedback during brainstorming sessions.

7.2. Legal and administrative assistance

- **Drafting contracts and legal documents:**
  Claude can be used as a tool to generate draft contracts, check the compliance of clauses or suggest clearer reformulations, thus facilitating the work of lawyers.
- **Administrative support:**
  In organizations, the model can automate the writing of reports, the management of internal correspondence or even the preparation of standardized administrative documents.

---

8. Conclusion

Claude's applications, and those of large language models in general, are deployed across a wide spectrum of sectors. In **customer service** , they offer responsive and personalized assistance, while in **writing** and **content creation** , they accelerate production and enrich creativity. In **education** , they become powerful learning and pedagogical support tools, and in fields such as health , finance , or **entertainment** , they optimize the analysis, synthesis, and communication of complex information.

This versatility illustrates how artificial intelligence, by integrating advanced text understanding and generation capabilities, is transforming business processes, improving operational efficiency and opening new avenues for innovation in virtually every area of activity.

Examples of task automation within companies.

1. Automation of administrative and management tasks

1.1. Mail processing and correspondence management

- **Automated email writing and response:**
  Advanced language models can analyze the content of incoming emails, identify requests, and generate tailored responses. For example, in a customer service department, a virtual assistant can sort and answer simple questions without human intervention.
- **Calendar management and meeting scheduling:**
  Automated tools integrated with digital calendars can suggest time slots, send invitations, and even organize meeting logistics, reducing the time spent on coordination.

1.2. Data entry and processing

- **Extracting data from documents:**
  OCR (optical character recognition) coupled with NLP models allows for the automatic extraction of information from invoices, contracts, or administrative forms. This speeds up the updating of internal databases and limits manual data entry errors.
- **Reporting and dashboard automation:**
  Systems can compile data from different departments (sales, production, human resources) to generate periodic reports. These tools transform raw data into visualizations and key indicators for decision-making.

2. Automation in customer service and customer relations

2.1. Chatbots and virtual assistants

- **Instant answers to frequently asked questions:**
  Chatbots, powered by language models such as Claude or GPT, provide 24/7 support, reducing the workload of human agents. They can handle simple requests such as checking balances, order status, or store hours.
- **Guidance and appointment scheduling:**
  In the health or beauty sectors, for example, virtual assistants can offer appointment slots based on availability and direct customers to the right department or specialist.

2.2. Personalization and loyalty

- **Customer behavior analysis:**
  Automation makes it possible to process large volumes of customer data to identify trends, personalize recommendations and adapt commercial offers.
- **Automated marketing campaign management:**
  Email and marketing automation tools send personalized messages based on purchase history or browsing behavior, thus strengthening engagement and loyalty.

3. Automation in production and logistics

3.1. Supply chain optimization

- **Demand forecasting and inventory management:**
  Machine learning algorithms analyze historical sales data, seasonal trends, and market signals to optimize inventory levels and avoid stockouts or overstocks.

- **Route planning and optimization:**
  In logistics, automated systems determine the most efficient routes for deliveries, reducing fuel costs and improving delivery times.

3.2. Automation of production

- **Collaborative robots (cobots):**
  In assembly lines, robots work alongside operators to perform repetitive tasks, such as assembling parts, packaging, or quality control.
- **Predictive maintenance:**
  Real-time analysis of machine data (vibrations, temperature, etc.) makes it possible to predict breakdowns and plan maintenance before a major failure occurs.

---

4. Automation in financial and legal fields

4.1. Automation of financial processes

- **Transaction processing and bank reconciliation:**
  Automated systems verify and reconcile transactions, detect anomalies and facilitate the production of financial statements, thus reducing the risk of human error and accelerating period-end closings.
- **Risk Analysis and Compliance:**
  AI algorithms examine financial data streams to identify suspicious patterns, aiding in fraud detection and compliance with applicable regulations (e.g., anti-money laundering).

4.2. Automation of legal tasks

- **Drafting legal documents:**
  AI-assisted tools can generate draft contracts, legal

clauses, or administrative documents, allowing lawyers to focus on strategic and personalized aspects.

- **Legal research:**
  Automated systems scan legal databases to extract precedents, analyze court decisions, or identify trends, facilitating case preparation and legal advice.

5. Automation in human resources

5.1. Recruitment and management of applications

- **Resume sorting and automated pre-screening:**
  Natural language processing tools analyze resumes to identify key skills and compare profiles with job requirements, thus accelerating the candidate pre-screening phase.
- **Chatbots for candidate communication:**
  These virtual assistants answer applicants' questions, schedule interviews, and provide updates on the status of the recruitment process.

5.2. Training and development

- **Personalized e-learning platforms:**
  Automation allows you to create training paths tailored to individual employee needs, with automatic assessments and recommendations for add-ons.
- **Performance tracking and feedback:**
  Automated systems collect and analyze performance data to provide regular feedback, identify areas for improvement, and plan targeted training.

6. Automation in research and development (R&D)

6.1. Information synthesis and technological monitoring

- **Analysis of scientific literature:**
  Language models automate the reading and synthesis of academic publications, facilitating technological monitoring and the discovery of information relevant to innovation.
- **Project management and technical documentation:**
  Automated tools help with writing and updating research documents, organizing technical meetings and centralizing acquired knowledge.

6.2. Prototyping and simulation

- **Idea generation and assisted brainstorming:**
  AI systems propose scenarios, innovation ideas or alternative solutions, thus stimulating creativity and efficiency in R&D projects.
- **Test Automation and Simulations:**
  In new product development, automated tools perform performance simulations, optimize parameters, and identify areas for improvement, thereby reducing testing and iteration cycles.

---

7. Other cross-cutting examples

7.1. Supplier relationship management

- **Automated negotiation:**
  Systems can analyze market conditions, generate contract proposals, and even negotiate certain

parameters with suppliers, facilitating supply chain management.

- **Order tracking and replenishment:**
  Automation allows you to track inventory levels in real time, automatically place orders when critical thresholds are reached, and coordinate deliveries.

7.2. Automation of internal communication

- **Smart intranets and virtual assistants:**
  Chatbots integrated into internal communication platforms answer employee questions, facilitate access to company information, and improve information flow.
- **Meeting Summarization and Task Management:**
  AI can transcribe and summarize meetings, assign tasks based on discussions, and track project progress, increasing coordination within teams.

Conclusion

Automating tasks within businesses offers a real revolution in business process management. Thanks to tools based on artificial intelligence, companies can:

- Reduce repetitive and administrative tasks to focus on high value-added activities.
- Improve the quality and speed of customer service with virtual assistants and chatbots.
- Optimize production, supply chain and financial management through real-time data analysis.
- Strengthen the productivity and efficiency of human resources, legal, commercial and R&D teams.
- Stimulate creativity and innovation by automating document research, information synthesis and idea generation.

These examples illustrate how automation, driven by advanced technologies such as large language models, is transforming the organization and competitiveness of businesses in a constantly evolving world. Each sector benefits from tailored approaches that reduce costs, increase operational accuracy, and deliver an enriched user experience, paving the way for a new era of intelligent and responsible productivity.

How Claude integrates into existing workflows (API, third-party integrations).

1. APIs as an integration gateway

1.1. REST and GraphQL Application Programming Interfaces (APIs)

- **Easy access:**
  Claude is typically accessible via REST or GraphQL APIs, allowing developers to call it from any HTTP-enabled environment.
- **Modular endpoints:**
  APIs offer specific endpoints for different functions, such as text generation, response synthesis, or even tone modulation. This allows businesses to choose precisely the services they need.

1.2. Authentication and quota management

- **Security and access control:**
  To protect usage and ensure confidentiality, access to Claude via its API is often protected by authentication keys and authentication mechanisms (OAuth, JWT, etc.).
- **Usage Management:**
  API providers implement quotas and pricing policies to manage usage based on business needs, allowing for scaling resource consumption and cost optimization.

---

2. Integration into existing business workflows

2.1. CRM systems and customer relationship management

- **Customer Service Automation:**
  Claude can be integrated with CRM tools (like Salesforce, HubSpot, Zoho) to power chatbots and virtual assistants that can answer customer questions, schedule appointments, or provide personalized recommendations.
- **Interaction Analysis:**
  Claude's API can process conversations, extract insights, and enrich customer profiles with behavioral data, helping sales teams better understand and anticipate needs.

2.2. Content management and publishing platforms

- **Automated Content Creation:**
  Marketing and editorial teams can connect Claude to their content management systems (CMS) like WordPress, Drupal, or proprietary solutions. The template can generate article drafts, summarize reports, or suggest eye-catching headlines, reducing production time.
- **Real-time Personalization:**
  Through API integration, Claude can be used to personalize the content displayed on a website based on the user's profile or browsing history, improving engagement and conversion.

2.3. Automation of writing and internal communications

- **Communication workflow:**
  Collaborative platforms like Slack, Microsoft Teams, or other intranet tools can integrate Claude to assist employees in drafting emails, meeting minutes, or administrative reports.
- **Internal chatbots:**
  By integrating Claude via an API, companies can deploy chatbots that answer frequently asked questions

from employees (for example, on internal policies, HR procedures, or IT requests), improving the fluidity of internal exchanges.

3. Integration with third-party systems and specialized platforms

3.1. Business intelligence and data analysis tools

- **Insight Extraction:**
  Claude can be integrated with Business Intelligence (BI) tools to analyze large amounts of text data, extract trends, generate summaries and create intelligent reports from raw data.
- **Interfacing with databases:**
  APIs allow Claude to interact directly with database systems or data warehouses, facilitating real-time updating of decision-making dashboards.

3.2. Mobile applications and conversational chatbots

- **Seamless User Experience:**
  Mobile app developers can integrate Claude to provide conversational assistants directly within their apps, providing a more intuitive and interactive user interface.
- **Omnichannel Integration:**
  By connecting Claude to messaging platforms (WhatsApp, Facebook Messenger, etc.), businesses can offer automated customer support and services across various channels, ensuring a consistent omnichannel experience.

3.3. ERP systems and automation of internal processes

- **Workflow optimization:**
  In integrated management environments (ERP such as SAP, Oracle), Claude can be called upon to automate tasks such as order management, demand forecasting or financial data synthesis.
- **Reduced manual tasks:**
  By automating report generation, data analysis and inter-departmental communication, Claude allows teams to focus on higher value-added tasks.

4. Flexibility and customization of integrations

4.1. Development of specific applications

- **Adaptation to business needs:**
  Claude's APIs offer flexibility that allows companies to develop tailor-made applications, integrating specific functionalities that meet the particularities of their sector or specific use cases.
- **Add-ons and plugins:**
  Plugins or add-ons can be designed for existing platforms, facilitating the integration of Claude without requiring a complete overhaul of existing systems.

4.2. Partner ecosystem and marketplaces

- **Third-party platforms:**
  API providers for major language models, like Anthropic, often work with technology partners who offer pre-built integrations for popular tools.
- **Marketplaces and SaaS solutions:**
  Specialized marketplaces bring together Claude-based solutions, allowing companies to quickly deploy applications without developing integration internally.

5. Benefits and challenges of integration

5.1. Advantages

- **Save time and reduce costs:**
  Automating tasks through Claude's integration reduces manual intervention, speeds up processes and achieves significant savings in terms of human resources.
- **Improved quality and consistency:**
  By standardizing responses and providing consistent support, Claude contributes to better quality of service and a consistent user experience.
- **Adaptability and scalability:**
  APIs allow for seamless integration into existing infrastructures, making it easier to expand services as the business grows or its needs change.

5.2. Challenges

- **Security and confidentiality:**
  Integrating Claude into sensitive workflows requires robust protocols to ensure data protection and compliance with regulations (GDPR, HIPAA, etc.).
- **Error Management and Resilience:**
  Like any API, Claude's API must be monitored and managed to ensure constant availability and effective error handling so as not to disrupt existing workflows.
- **Customization without performance loss:**
  Adapting Claude to the specificities of each company sometimes requires fine tuning and customization, which can complicate deployment without affecting overall performance.

6. Conclusion

Claude's integration into existing workflows relies on a robust and flexible API architecture, allowing businesses to leverage the advanced capabilities of this large language model in various areas: customer service, content management, internal process automation, and much more.
By connecting to CRM systems, ERP, BI platforms, mobile applications, and other specialized tools, Claude offers a versatile and scalable solution that transforms business processes. While delivering significant benefits in terms of productivity and quality of service, this integration requires careful attention to security, customization, and error handling to ensure a seamless experience that meets end-user expectations.

Thus, Claude positions itself not only as a powerful text generation engine, but also as a key element in optimizing business workflows, facilitating a harmonious and responsible digital transformation.

Chapter 6: Dialogue and interaction with Claude

"Prompting" process□: how to ask the right questions to get relevant answers .

1. Understand "Prompting" and its importance

1.1. Definition and role

- **Prompting** is how you "invite" the model to generate a response by providing it with context or a question.
- The wording of the prompt directly influences the quality, accuracy and relevance of the responses generated.
- A good prompt guides the model, limits ambiguity, and allows language comprehension capabilities to be fully exploited.

1.2. Importance in interaction with LLMs

- Language models, despite their size and performance, lack intrinsic understanding like humans. Their "knowledge" is derived from statistics on huge text corpora.
- A well-designed prompt helps **direct the model's attention** to the relevant information and structures the response in a coherent manner.
- In the business context, effective prompting can transform the user experience by delivering more accurate, tailored, and reliable results.

2. Strategies for formulating effective prompts

2.1. Precision and context

- **Specificity:**
  Specifying the topic or field helps avoid overly generic answers. For example, instead of asking "Explain biology," it's better to ask "Explain how photosynthesis allows plants to convert light into energy."
- **Detailed context:**
  Providing contextual information, such as examples, definitions, or constraints, helps the model better understand the request.
  - For example, asking "Can you give me three concrete examples of automation in the banking sector, emphasizing the impact on cost reduction and improved customer service?" guides the model to provide structured and relevant answers.

2.2. Structuring the prompt

- **Use lists or multiple questions:**
  Dividing the prompt into sub-questions or points to be addressed helps clarify expectations.
  - Example: "1. What are the main stages of photosynthesis? 2. What enzymes are involved? 3. How do these processes influence plant growth?"
- **Frame the response format:**
  Explicitly requesting a particular format (list, structured paragraph, summary) helps the model organize its output in a readable and usable way.
  - Example: "Give me a five-point summary of the technological challenges in AI."

2.3. Use of explicit instructions

- **Clear instructions:**
  Instructions should specify the desired style, tone, and depth.
    - Example: "Write an informative and detailed article on the history of artificial intelligence, adopting an academic tone and citing specific examples."
- **Examples and counterexamples:**
  Providing an example of an expected response or indicating what to avoid helps further refine the model's behavior.

---

3. Advanced prompting techniques

3.1. Using "chain-of-thought"

- **Encourage step-by-step thinking:**
  Asking the model to explain its reasoning step by step can improve the quality of answers, especially for complex tasks or logic problems.
    - Example: "Describe, step by step, how to solve a quadratic equation, explaining each mathematical manipulation."

3.2. Modulation via "role prompts"

- **Adopt a specific perspective:**
  Inviting the model to respond by putting themselves in the shoes of an expert or advisor allows for more specialized responses.
    - Example: "As an economics expert, explain the effects of expansionary monetary policy on inflation."

3.3. Adjusting length and level of detail

- **Define length constraints:**
  Specifying whether the response should be short and concise or detailed and exhaustive helps to frame the response.
    - Example: "Give me a 200-word summary of the Industrial Revolution, highlighting the major technological changes."
- **Request clarification or further development:**
  A prompt can be enriched by a request for clarification on certain points, encouraging the model to delve deeper into a given subject.

---

4. Good practices and pitfalls to avoid

4.1. Clarity and conciseness

- **Avoid ambiguity:**
  Prompts should be worded clearly and concisely to limit multiple interpretations.
- **Rephrase if necessary:**
  If the initial response is vague or off-topic, it may be helpful to rephrase or further clarify the prompt.

4.2. Test and iterate

- **Iterative process:**
  Designing effective prompts often requires multiple trials. Adjusting the wording based on responses allows for gradual refinement of the prompt.
- **Collect feedback:**
  In a professional environment, analyzing responses and obtaining user feedback helps improve the quality of prompts.

4.3. Sensitivity to model biases

- **Recognize limitations:**
  Even with a good prompt, responses may reflect biases present in the model.
- **Apply filters or safety instructions:**
  It is often necessary to include warnings or constraints to avoid inappropriate content, especially on sensitive topics.

---

5. Concrete examples of effective prompts

Example 1: Customer service application

- **Simple prompt:** "Tell me how to cancel a reservation online."
- **Improved Prompt:** "As an airline customer service assistant, describe in five detailed steps the procedure for canceling a reservation online, specifying the conditions and possible refunds."

Example 2: Application in writing

- **Simple prompt:** "Write an article about climate change."
- **Improved Prompt:** "Write an 800-word paper on climate change, focusing on anthropogenic causes, consequences for the global ecosystem, and possible solutions. Use an informative tone and cite recent data to illustrate your points."

Example 3: Application in education

- **Simple Prompt:** "Explain photosynthesis."
- **Improved Prompt:** "As a biology teacher for high school students, explain photosynthesis in a clear and structured manner. Describe the chemical reactions involved, the organelles involved, and the importance

of this process for the environment. Use concrete
examples to illustrate your explanations."

---

6. Conclusion

The **prompting process** is an essential component for taking
full advantage of the capabilities of large language models. By
asking clear, detailed, and structured questions, it is possible to
obtain answers that precisely meet user needs, whether in a
professional, educational, or creative context.
To achieve this, it is crucial to:

- **Provide accurate context** and clear instructions,
- **Structure the prompt** to guide the model optimally,
- **Use advanced techniques** like chain-of-thought and
  role prompts,
- **Iterate and adjust** based on feedback and observed
  performance.

Thus, the success of prompting relies on a balance between
technical rigor and creativity in formulation, allowing the full
potential of tools like Claude to be exploited to generate
relevant, useful responses adapted to various needs.

Concrete demonstrations, tips and best practices for interaction.

1. Concrete demonstrations of successful interactions

1.1. Examples of prompts adapted to specific use cases

- **Customer Service:**
  Simple example: "How can I track my order?"
  Improved example: "As a customer service assistant for an online store, describe in 5 steps how a customer can check the status of their order using their tracking number. Also mention update times and solutions in case of problems."
  Impact: This prompt gives the template a specific context (customer service, online store) and structures the response in several steps, which improves the clarity and relevance of the information provided.
- **Marketing Content Writing:**
  Simple example: "Write an article about sustainability."
  Improved example: "As a digital marketing copywriter, write a 600-word article about sustainability, emphasizing technological innovations that are driving the energy transition. Use an engaging tone and include real-life examples of companies pioneering this field."
  Impact: The detailed prompt guides the template on the expected length, tone, and examples, resulting in more focused and professional content.
- **Teaching and Tutoring:**
  Simple example: "Explain photosynthesis."
  Improved example: "As a high school biology teacher, explain photosynthesis by detailing the chemical reactions involved, the role of chloroplasts, and the importance of this process to the ecosystem. Use simple analogies to facilitate student understanding."

Impact: Here, the educational context and desired level of detail help the model adapt its vocabulary and use pedagogically relevant examples.

1.2. Interaction in dialogue and contextualization

- **Maintaining context in a conversation:**
  During a multi-turn exchange, it's important to briefly provide context or reference previously discussed points.
  Example: "To continue our discussion on sustainable development, can you elaborate on how green technologies influence the reduction of CO_2 emissions in heavy industries?"
  Tip: Referencing previous messages allows the model to better understand the evolution of the conversation and provide a coherent response.
- **Using iterative instructions:**
  It is possible to gradually refine the request if the initial response is not entirely satisfactory.
  Example: After an initial response that is too general, ask "Can you specify the impacts on the supply chain and give specific examples of companies that have implemented these technologies?"
  Tip: This iterative method allows you to clarify expectations and guide the model towards a more complete and detailed response.

2. Tips for improving interaction with language models

2.1. Structure the request

- **Use numbered or bulleted lists:**
  Formulating questions in multiple parts or sub-questions helps the model structure their response

clearly.

Example: "Can you give me:
1. A concise definition of deep learning,
2. An example of application in image recognition,
3. The main challenges of training neural networks?

- **Frame the response format:**
  If a particular format is desired (e.g., 3-point summary, comparison table, etc.), indicating it in the prompt allows for an organized and easy-to-use response.

2.2. Specify the tone and style

- **Adapt the tone to the target audience:**
  Specifying whether the response should be formal, technical, educational, or friendly allows the model to choose the appropriate vocabulary and style.
  Example: "Adopt an academic and formal tone to explain…" or "Use a simple and accessible style to describe…"
- **Provide examples of expected answers:**
  Briefly stating what you expect helps guide the model.
  Example: "I am looking for a structured explanation with concrete examples, similar to a scientific journal article."

2.3. Use "role prompts"

- **Position yourself as an expert or advisor:**
  By asking the model to respond as if it were a specialist in a field, you can obtain more specific answers.
  Example: "As an expert in artificial intelligence, describe the advantages and limitations of convolutional neural networks in image recognition."
- **Change perspective depending on the context:**
  To get a response from different angles, you can ask for multiple viewpoints (e.g., scientific, business, ethical).

Example: "Explain first from a technical perspective, then from a business perspective, the impact of AI technologies on the healthcare sector."

---

3. Best practices for continuous interaction

3.1. Iteration and adjustment

- **Repeat or rephrase the request if necessary:**
  If the initial response does not meet expectations, it is wise to rephrase the prompt by adding more details or clarifying certain points.
- **Collect user feedback:**
  In a professional usage context, testing different formulations and collecting feedback from end users allows prompts to be optimized empirically.

3.2. Document best practices

- **Create a library of effective prompts:**
  Companies can set up internal databases of prompts that have performed well for different use cases.
- **Train teams on the principles of prompting:**
  Training internal users (writers, analysts, developers) to formulate clear and structured prompts helps optimize the use of language models and improve the quality of responses.

3.3. Monitor and evaluate interactions

- **Analyzing model responses:**
  Implementing quality indicators (relevance, consistency, length, accuracy) and regularly evaluating interactions helps identify areas for improvement.
- **Test with varied scenarios:**
  It is recommended to use a wide range of prompts

covering different domains and levels of complexity to ensure that the model responds satisfactorily in various contexts.

---

4. Conclusion

The demonstration process, tips, and best practices for interacting with language models such as Claude rely on precise, structured, and contextual formulation of prompts. By applying these methods, it is possible to:

- Guide the model to obtain clear, detailed answers tailored to specific needs,
- Maintain smooth and coherent interaction over multiple conversation turns,
- Optimize the quality of results through successive iterations and documentation of best practices.

In short, mastering the art of prompting not only improves the tool's efficiency, but also allows you to fully exploit the potential of language models in a variety of applications, ranging from customer service to content creation, education, and many other fields. This dynamic and iterative approach is part of a continuous improvement process, essential for getting the most out of artificial intelligence technologies.

Claude's limitations and tips for working around or resolving common issues.

1. Limitations inherent in language models

1.1. Hallucinations and inaccuracies

- **Definition:**
  Claude, like other LLMs, can sometimes generate erroneous or fabricated information, a phenomenon commonly referred to as "hallucination."
- **Causes:**
  - Reliance on huge textual corpora which themselves contain errors or approximations.
  - Statistical modeling that favors apparent consistency over factual truth.
- **Consequences :**
  - Imprecise answers, which can be misleading in critical contexts (medical, legal, scientific).

1.2. Sensitivity to formulations and lack of robustness

- **Prompt variability:**
  Claude's response can vary significantly depending on the wording of the prompt.
- **Multi-turn consistency issues:**
  In extended conversations, the model may lose context or give inconsistent responses relative to previously discussed information.
- **Uncertainty in specialized areas:**
  For specific questions or very technical areas, Claude can sometimes give approximate answers or lack depth.

1.3. Limits of context and memory

- **Limited context window:**
  Even though Claude is designed to handle a large number of tokens, there is a limit on the amount of information the model can "retain" simultaneously.
- **Context degradation effect:**
  When the conversation moves beyond the context window, initial information may be forgotten or misinterpreted.

1.4. Biases and ethical constraints

- **Inherited data biases:**
  Claude may reflect stereotypes or biases present in the training data, despite filtering and alignment mechanisms.
- **Excessive censorship or limitation of freedom of expression:**
  Measures put in place to prevent the generation of inappropriate content can sometimes lead to overly strict censorship, limiting the richness of responses in certain areas.

2. Tips and strategies to work around or resolve these issues

2.1. To manage hallucinations and inaccuracies

- **Source verification:**
  Always verify important information with reliable sources. For example, for scientific or technical data, consult research articles or recognized publications.
- **Use clarification prompts:**
  If the answer seems questionable, asking the model to detail their reasoning or provide references can help identify errors.

- **Iteration and Reformulation:**
  If the answer is imprecise, rewording the prompt by including more context or asking specific questions can lead to a more rigorous answer.

2.2. To improve the consistency and robustness of responses

- **Clear contextualization:**
  In extended dialogues, briefly restating key points previously covered in each new prompt helps maintain consistency.
- **Multi-step prompts:**
  Dividing complex requests into multiple sub-questions allows for more structured and detailed responses.
- **Use role prompts:**
  Asking the model to respond by putting themselves in the role of an expert can help elicit more targeted and robust responses.

2.3. To bypass the pop-up window limitations

- **Periodic Summarization:**
  During long conversations, asking Claude to summarize the key points regularly helps to "refresh" the context and retain important information.
- **Segment the conversation:**
  Dividing interactions into independent modules and linking them with summaries allows you to handle complex tasks without losing the thread of information.

2.4. To mitigate bias and manage ethical constraints

- **Prompt Curation and Adjustment:**
  When addressing sensitive topics, it is important to formulate prompts in a neutral and balanced manner.
- **Use of explicit filters:**
  Including specific instructions in the prompt to avoid

certain content or stereotypes can help reduce the manifestation of bias.
- **Continuous feedback:**
Incorporating a feedback system where users flag biased or inappropriate responses allows for model refinement and adjustment of alignment parameters.

---

3. Best practices for optimal interaction with Claude

3.1. Iteration and A/B testing

- **Test different prompt formulations** and compare responses to identify those that give the most consistent and accurate results.
- **Documenting prompting best practices** within the company allows for internal knowledge sharing and standardization of the model's use.

3.2. Personalization and contextual adjustments

- **Adapt the prompt according to the target audience** : for technical content, use specialized vocabulary; for educational content, prioritize simplicity and pedagogy.
- **Use contextual guides** that clarify expectations, such as examples of expected responses, to accurately direct the model.

3.3. Continuous monitoring and readjustment

- **Implement monitoring systems** to track performance and possible deviations from the model, thus enabling rapid response in the event of a problem.
- **Conduct regular audits** by internal or external teams (red teams) to identify and correct unwanted behavior.

4. Conclusion

Although Claude offers impressive capabilities for generating and processing language, it has inherent limitations such as hallucinations, sensitivity to wording, a limited contextual window, and potential biases. To circumvent these issues, several strategies can be implemented:

- **Verification of information** by external sources and iteration of prompts to reduce errors.
- **Clear structuring of interactions** and use of advanced prompting techniques to improve consistency.
- **Context segmentation** and regular summaries to overcome the limitations of long-term memory.
- **Adjusting instructions** to mitigate bias and ensure an ethical and balanced response.

Adopting these best practices not only improves the quality of Claude's responses, but also optimizes its integration into various professional applications, while ensuring responsible and secure use of artificial intelligence technologies.

Chapter 7: Anthropic's Contributions to AI Ethics

Anthropic's approach to transparency and reducing misinformation.

1. Philosophical and objective foundations

1.1. An ethical and responsible mission

- **Long-term vision:** Anthropic places safety and ethics at the heart of its mission, believing that the development of AI must benefit society as a whole. The company's goal is to reduce the risk of abuse (disinformation, bias, harmful content) while promoting AI that supports transparency.
- **Alignment with human values:** The goal is for AI systems, like Claude, to reflect society's principles and values—respect, fairness, and truthfulness—to limit the spread of false or misleading information.

1.2. The need for transparency

- **Open communication about methods:** Anthropic is committed to sharing, wherever possible, the broad outlines of its filtering, training, and alignment methods. This transparency aims to strengthen the trust of users, regulators, and the scientific community.
- **Responsibility and Accountability:** By outlining guiding principles and internal protocols (such as "Constitutional AI"), Anthropic seeks to establish standards of AI governance that can be verified and constructively criticized.

2. Technical mechanisms for reducing disinformation

2.1. The "Constitutional AI" approach

- **Defining a constitution for the model:** Anthropic is developing an approach in which the model is guided by an explicit set of ethical rules or principles—its "constitution." These rules serve as a framework for evaluating and moderating the responses generated, in order to limit misinformation and potentially harmful content.
- **Reinforced learning with human feedback (RLHF):** In fine-tuning, human annotators evaluate the model's responses. Feedback is used to reorient the model's behavior, punishing erroneous or misleading responses and reinforcing those that follow established principles.

2.2. Data filtering and curation

- **Rigorous source selection:** During the pre-training phase, Anthropic performs extensive filtering of the corpora used, eliminating as much as possible sources known to propagate erroneous, biased or low-quality information.
- **Controlling inherent bias:** The company implements detection systems to identify and mitigate biases present in training data, thereby minimizing the risk that the model will reproduce or amplify factual errors or stereotypes.

2.3. Evaluation protocols and audits

- **Robustness testing:** Anthropic regularly organizes testing sessions, often called "red team tests," where internal or external teams seek to push the model to its limits to identify potential flaws in terms of misinformation or inappropriate content.

- **Continuous updating of moderation mechanisms:** Based on feedback from these audits, filtering algorithms and constitution rules are regularly reassessed and improved to remain relevant in the face of changing discourse and societal contexts.

3. Transparency in communication and interaction with the community

3.1. Publication of research and methods

- **Sharing scientific advances:** Anthropic regularly publishes articles and technical reports that detail, at least partially, the methods implemented for model alignment and moderation. These publications contribute to academic discussion and allow researchers to compare and challenge existing approaches.
- **Participation in forums and conferences:** The company is actively involved in international conferences and working groups on AI security and ethics, thus promoting the exchange of best practices and transparency on its approaches.

3.2. Accessible documentation and user guides

- **Educational Resources:** Anthropic offers guides, documentation, and examples of how to use its APIs and templates to help developers understand the built-in moderation principles. These resources include how to formulate prompts to minimize the risk of generating misinformation.
- **Transparency about limitations:** In addition to sharing its successes, the company also communicates about the current limitations of its models, urging users

to be vigilant and combine AI with human verification, especially in sensitive or critical areas.

---

4. Collaboration and engagement with stakeholders

4.1. Partnerships with institutions and NGOs

- **Joint Initiatives:** Anthropic collaborates with regulators, digital rights groups, and universities to develop ethical and technical standards to reduce misinformation.
- **Independent audits:** By partnering with external experts, the company encourages independent audits that validate its moderation and alignment processes, thus strengthening the credibility of its approaches.

4.2. Dialogue with the community

- **Public Feedback:** By inviting users to flag problematic answers and incorporating this feedback into future iterations, Anthropic takes a collaborative approach to continually improving the quality and reliability of its models.
- **Proactive Transparency:** The company seeks to be proactive in communicating about challenges encountered, improvements made and future prospects to combat disinformation, in order to build a climate of trust with its customers and partners.

---

5. Persistent challenges and opportunities for improvement

5.1. Information complexity and scalability

- **Evolving narratives:** Disinformation and bias evolve over time and across sociopolitical contexts. Moderation systems must therefore be constantly updated to remain effective in the face of new forms of misleading or extremist discourse.
- **Scalability of solutions:** As models expand and their use becomes more widespread, maintaining full transparency and fine-grained moderation remains a technical and organizational challenge.

5.2. Balance between security and freedom of expression

- **Risks of excessive censorship:** Overly strict moderation can prevent the dissemination of legitimate information or nuance complex debates. The goal is to strike a balance that protects against misinformation without unduly restricting freedom of expression.
- **Adaptation to local contexts:** Cultural and legal norms vary from country to country. Anthropic must design modular mechanisms that allow moderation rules to be adapted to the specific contexts of end users.

6. Conclusion

Anthropic's approach to transparency and reducing misinformation revolves around several key areas:

- **Integration of a "Constitutional AI"** which defines a strict ethical framework for the behavior of the models,
- **Rigorous data filtering and curation** to limit the contribution of erroneous content from the outset,
- **Advanced feedback and moderation mechanisms** (including RLHF and red team audits) to continuously adjust the model,

- **Open communication and partnerships** with the scientific community and regulators, in order to promote responsible practices.

By adopting this multifaceted strategy, Anthropic is not only working to reduce the spread of misinformation, but also to build an AI ecosystem that inspires trust and can serve as an example for the entire industry. This approach, combining technical innovation and ethical commitment, aims to ensure that artificial intelligence technologies are deployed in a way that enhances the common good, while minimizing the risks inherent in their use.

Policies and protocols in place to prevent malicious use of AI.

1. Context and issues

1.1. Risks associated with malicious use

- **Disinformation and Manipulation:**
  Language models, by generating convincing text, can be misused to produce and disseminate false information, influence political opinions or amplify extremist narratives.
- **Hateful and discriminatory content:**
  Without strict supervision, AI can reproduce or even reinforce stereotypes, spread hateful messages or encourage discriminatory behavior.
- **Criminal exploitation:**
  Malicious actors could use AI to automate phishing campaigns, generate fraudulent emails, or bypass security systems.

1.2. Importance of prevention policies

- **Social Responsibility:**
  Companies that develop and deploy AI models must act responsibly to protect users and society as a whole.
- **Trust and Adoption:**
  Implementing security measures builds trust among users, partners and regulators, thereby promoting wider and ethical adoption of these technologies.

---

2. Internal policies and technical protocols

2.1. Data filtering and curation

- **Rigorous source selection:**
  From the pre-training phase, the data corpus is carefully filtered to eliminate explicitly violent, hateful or misleading content.
- **Bias Reduction:**
  Bias detection and correction methods are applied to prevent models from reproducing unwanted stereotypes or biases.

2.2. "Constitutional AI" approach

- **Defining an ethical framework:**
  The "Constitutional AI" strategy consists of providing the model with a set of ethical rules, a sort of internal charter that guides its behavior during inference.
- **Explicit guidelines:**
  These rules include refusing to generate violent, hateful, or illegal content, while requiring neutrality and accuracy in the responses provided.

2.3. Reinforcement by supervised learning and human feedback

- **RLHF (Reinforcement Learning from Human Feedback):**
  The fine-tuning process incorporates human evaluations that flag unwanted model behaviors. This feedback allows parameters to be adjusted to reinforce ethically compliant responses and discourage deviations.
- **Continuous Iterations and Adjustments:**
  The model is regularly retrained and adjusted based on user feedback and internal audits, ensuring continuous improvement in managing potentially malicious content.

2.4. Real-time moderation protocols

- **Automatic detection systems:**
  Specialized algorithms analyze incoming requests and generated responses in real time to detect any risky content.
- **Refusal or Redirection:**
  If problematic content is detected, the model can be programmed to refuse to respond or to redirect the conversation to a neutral and safe response.

3. Audits, red teaming and external supervision

3.1. Regular internal audits

- **Robustness tests:**
  Development teams perform internal audits by subjecting the model to critical scenarios to identify weak points and risks of deviation.
- **Measuring ethical performance:**
  Specific indicators, such as the rate of refusal of sensitive content or the frequency of biased responses, are monitored to assess the effectiveness of moderation measures.

3.2. Red teaming and independent audits

- **Hiring external experts:**
  Red teams (groups of specialized testers) are hired to try to bypass security measures and cause failures in the system.
- **Feedback and correction:**
  The results of these tests make it possible to identify unforeseen flaws and make rapid corrections, thus strengthening the model's resilience against malicious use.

3.3. Collaboration with regulators and the community

- **Institutional Partnerships:**
  Anthropic collaborates with regulatory bodies and research groups to share best practices and contribute to the development of international standards for ethical AI.
- **Transparency on protocols:**
  By participating in conferences and publishing reports, the company commits to being transparent about the policies in place, thus facilitating trust and acceptance of its technologies.

---

4. Additional measures and management of evolving risks

4.1. Adaptability and continuous updates

- **Monitoring societal developments:**
  Moderation policies must adapt to changes in public discourse and new modes of malicious exploitation. Anthropic implements processes for regularly reviewing internal rules.
- **Integration of user feedback:**
  Direct feedback from users and partners makes it possible to detect unforeseen uses and quickly adjust protocols to limit risks.

4.2. Crisis management and emergency procedures

- **Contingency plans:**
  In the event of large-scale misuse being detected, emergency procedures are in place to temporarily interrupt access to the model or deploy security updates.

- **Transparent communication:**
  In the event of a breach, it is essential to quickly inform stakeholders and describe the steps taken to correct the problem in order to maintain trust.

---

5. Conclusion

The policies and protocols implemented to prevent malicious use of AI illustrate a proactive and multifaceted approach. They are based on several essential pillars:

- **Rigorous data curation and filtering** to limit the initial intake of toxic or biased content.
- **The "Constitutional AI" approach** which establishes a clear ethical framework to guide the model's responses.
- **Learning from human feedback and fine-tuning iterations,** which allow us to correct drifts and continuously improve the model's behavior.
- **Internal audits and red teaming,** which identify potential vulnerabilities and strengthen resilience against malicious exploitation attempts.
- **Collaboration with regulators and the scientific community** to promote universal standards and ensure transparency of processes.

By adopting this integrated approach, Anthropic seeks to minimize the risks associated with malicious uses of AI while promoting responsible and ethical use of its technologies, thereby ensuring they serve the common good and strengthen trust in artificial intelligence.

Dialogue with the scientific community and the public to promote responsible AI.

1. Engagement with the scientific community

1.1. Active participation in conferences and seminars

- **Presentations and publications** :
  Anthropic regularly participates in international conferences (NeurIPS, ICML, ICLR, AAAI, etc.) where its researchers present work on the alignment, moderation, and safety of language models. These presentations provide an opportunity to share technical advances and discuss ethical issues.
- **Workshops and Working Groups** :
  The company organizes or co-organizes specialized workshops that bring together researchers, practitioners, and regulators to discuss best practices in AI safety, bias reduction, and ethical governance.

1.2. Collaboration with academic and research institutions

- **Collaborative Research Projects** :
  Anthropic works in partnership with universities and research centers to develop evaluation protocols and tools to measure the robustness and alignment of AI models.
- **Sharing results and data** :
  While some aspects remain proprietary, the company regularly publishes articles and technical reports on platforms such as arXiv. These publications allow the scientific community to reproduce results, suggest improvements, and contribute to the evolution of standards.

- **Open source initiatives** :
  Collaboration sometimes results in the provision of open source tools and libraries, thus promoting the adoption of common standards and transparency of methods.

2. Dialogue with the public and awareness raising

2.1. Transparent communication on issues and methods

- **Blogs and Reports** :
  Anthropic publishes blog posts, white papers, and activity reports that detail not only technical advances, but also ethical challenges and measures taken to ensure responsible AI.
- **Transparency about limitations** :
  The company doesn't try to hide the limitations of its models. Instead, it communicates openly about potential risks, existing biases, and areas for improvement, inviting the public to critically reflect on the use of AI.

2.2. Discussion forums and public consultations

- **Collaborative platforms** :
  Anthropic participates in forums, webinars and discussion panels that bring together not only technical experts, but also representatives of the general public, regulators and non-governmental organizations.
- **Gathering feedback** :
  By soliciting opinions and feedback from users and the public, the company can adapt its strategies and improve its tools. These exchanges allow for a better

understanding of societal concerns and the integration of diverse perspectives into AI development.

2.3. Education and popularization

- **Educational initiatives** :
  To demystify artificial intelligence, Anthropic engages in science outreach programs, organizing workshops and conferences aimed at a non-specialist audience.
- **Educational materials** :
  The company offers accessible resources, such as tutorials, explainer videos, and how-to guides, to help the public understand how AI works, its limitations, and how it can be used ethically.

---

3. Promotion of standards and an ethical framework

3.1. Contributions to debates on AI regulation

- **Participation in regulatory consultations** :
  Anthropic collaborates with government bodies and international organizations to define standards and regulations to govern the development and use of AI.
- **Developing codes of conduct** :
  By participating in cross-industry working groups, the company contributes to the development of guidelines and codes of conduct intended to ensure that AI is deployed responsibly and fairly.

3.2. Partnerships with other players in the sector

- **Cross-company initiatives** :
  To create a responsible AI ecosystem, Anthropic collaborates with other companies and research labs. These partnerships aim to share best practices,

harmonize security protocols, and promote transparency throughout the development chain.
- **Think Tanks and Consortia** :
  The company is involved in consortia that bring together experts in ethics, law, technology and social sciences to discuss the societal impacts of AI and propose solutions adapted to contemporary challenges.

4. Challenges and prospects for development

4.1. Managing the complexity of issues

- **Rapidly evolving technologies** :
  The field of AI is evolving rapidly, and transparency and ethics challenges are evolving with new innovations. Anthropic must therefore constantly update its practices and adapt to newly identified risks.
- **Diversity of opinions and cultural contexts** :
  Promoting responsible AI must take into account the plurality of values and norms across the world. This involves developing modular mechanisms that can be adapted to different cultural and regulatory contexts.

4.2. Pursue collaborative innovation

- **Strengthening interdisciplinary exchanges** :
  The complexity of ethical questions related to AI requires an interdisciplinary approach involving technicians, philosophers, lawyers and sociologists.
- **Proactive Transparency** :
  By continuing to publish research and invite dialogue, Anthropic hopes not only to improve its own systems, but also to inspire responsible practices across the industry.

5. Conclusion

Dialogue with the scientific community and the public is a central pillar of Anthropic's approach to promoting responsible AI. Through open communication, collaborative partnerships, outreach initiatives, and active participation in regulatory debates, the company seeks to:

- **Building trust** in AI by sharing its methods and being transparent about its challenges.
- **Encourage an interdisciplinary exchange** that allows technologies to be adapted to societal and cultural values.
- **Contribute to the development of universal standards** and codes of conduct that govern the ethical development and use of AI.

By adopting this strategy, Anthropic demonstrates its commitment to putting AI research and development at the service of the common good, while anticipating and mitigating the risks associated with a powerful and constantly evolving technology.

Chapter 8: The ecosystem around Claude

Key partnerships, collaborations with other companies or research organizations.

1. Objectives and challenges of partnerships

1.1. Pooling of technical and ethical expertise

- **Complementary skills:**
  Partnerships allow Anthropic to combine its expertise in artificial intelligence with the specialized knowledge of other stakeholders (universities, research centers, technology companies). This fosters innovation by integrating diverse perspectives and confronting technical approaches with in-depth ethical reflections.
- **Deepening fundamental research:**
  Collaboration with academic institutions offers the opportunity to explore new methodologies, develop innovative algorithms, and refine language model moderation and alignment techniques.

1.2. Resource sharing and cost reduction

- **Access to advanced computing infrastructure:**
  Partnerships with companies with significant computing capacity or supercomputing centers allow Anthropic to benefit from an infrastructure suitable for training large models.
- **Funding and logistical support:**
  Collaborations with research organizations and strategic companies also help share the costs associated with developing AI technologies, while ensuring logistical and financial support for large-scale projects.

1.3. Promotion of responsible and secure AI

- **Alignment with common ethical standards:**
  By partnering with organizations dedicated to AI safety
  and ethics, Anthropic is engaging in a process of co-
  constructing standards and best practices that benefit
  the entire industry.
- **Transparency and collaborative governance:**
  Partnerships promote the dissemination of information,
  the joint publication of research results and the
  establishment of external audit mechanisms, thus
  contributing to more transparent and accountable
  governance in the AI industry.

---

2. Terms of collaboration

2.1. Joint research projects

- **Collaborative initiatives in fundamental research:**
  Anthropic partners with universities and research
  centers to conduct studies on crucial topics such as
  model alignment, bias reduction, and optimization of
  Transformer architectures. These joint projects allow
  for the publication of scientific papers, presentation of
  results at international conferences, and exchange of
  cutting-edge knowledge.
- **Cross-industry partnerships:**
  Collaborations are also being established with other
  technology companies, enabling the development of
  industrial applications of AI. For example, joint
  projects may aim to integrate language models into
  customer service platforms or recommendation
  systems, combining Anthropic's technical expertise
  with its partners' market knowledge.

2.2. Strategic partnerships and consortia

- **Collaboration with regulators and NGOs:**
  To anticipate and regulate malicious uses of AI, Anthropic participates in cross-sector working groups, such as the Partnership on AI, where companies, governments, and non-governmental organizations come together to define common ethical standards and security protocols.
- **Participation in research consortia:**
  By participating in consortia and collaborative research projects (sometimes funded by public agencies or private foundations), Anthropic contributes to the creation of a shared framework for the responsible development of AI technologies.

2.3. Open source initiatives and technology sharing

- **Contributions to open source projects:**
  While some aspects of its technologies remain proprietary, Anthropic, like many companies in the industry, has demonstrated a willingness to share certain libraries, tools, and methodologies. These contributions help strengthen the AI ecosystem and accelerate innovation globally.
- **Collaborations with development platforms:**
  By partnering with players like GitHub or other technology collaboration platforms, Anthropic facilitates the integration of its tools into third-party projects, thus promoting wider dissemination and progressive adoption of its technologies.

3. Concrete examples of partnerships and collaborations

3.1. Academic collaborations

- **Prestigious Institutions:**
  Partnerships with universities such as MIT, Stanford, and Carnegie Mellon give Anthropic access to cutting-edge research labs and the benefit of the work of renowned AI researchers. These collaborations often result in joint publications and funded research projects.
- **Thesis projects and training programs:**
  Anthropic's commitment to training new generations of researchers is demonstrated through the funding of theses, the organization of seminars and participation in academic exchange programs.

3.2. Industrial partnerships

- **Integration into technology ecosystems:**
  Major technology companies are collaborating with Anthropic to integrate advanced language models into their services. For example, in the cloud computing sector, partnerships enable AI solutions to be offered via secure and scalable APIs.
- **Product co-development:**
  Joint initiatives with companies specializing in cybersecurity, healthcare or finance can lead to the creation of products integrating AI modules, optimized to meet the specific needs of these sectors.

3.3. Intersectoral projects and international consortia

- **International AI Standards:**
  By participating in consortia bringing together public and private actors, Anthropic contributes to the development of international norms and standards that govern the use of AI, ensuring that these technologies are deployed in a safe, ethical and responsible manner.
- **Red teaming and collaborative security initiatives:**
  Collaboration with organizations specializing in IT

security allows for external audits to be carried out, the robustness of systems to be tested, and areas for improvement to be identified to prevent malicious use.

4. Impacts and benefits of partnerships

4.1. Acceleration of innovation

- **Knowledge transfer:**
  Collaborations foster a constant exchange of knowledge, ideas and expertise, which accelerates the development of new technologies and helps overcome technical and ethical challenges more quickly.
- **Technological synergies:**
  The pooling of resources (infrastructure, financing, expertise) makes it possible to develop more complex and efficient solutions that would not be possible to achieve alone.

4.2. Strengthening credibility and trust

- **Transparency and shared governance:**
  By partnering with recognized institutions and jointly publishing scientific work, Anthropic strengthens the credibility of its approaches and helps build trust among users and regulators.
- **Ethical Leadership:**
  By actively participating in debates on AI regulation and engaging in collaborative security initiatives, the company positions itself as a responsible leader in the sector, setting an example in terms of transparency and ethical alignment.

5. Conclusion

Key partnerships and collaborations with other companies and research organizations are a fundamental pillar of Anthropic's strategy to develop advanced and responsible artificial intelligence. By combining the strengths of academic research, industrial expertise, and cross-sector initiatives, Anthropic succeeds in:

- **Accelerate innovation** through a synergy of skills and resources,
- **Strengthening the safety** and ethics of AI technologies through audits, collaborative projects and contributions to international standards,
- **Promote transparency** and open dialogue with the scientific community, regulators and the general public.

These partnerships not only enable the development of cutting-edge products, but also create a sustainable and responsible framework for the entire artificial intelligence industry, ensuring that technological advances are used for the common good and aligned with universal ethical values.

The developer and user community: roles, feedback, forums, etc.

1. Role and importance of the community

1.1. Co-construction and open innovation

- **Knowledge sharing and best practices:**
  Developers and researchers share their discoveries, scripts, and experiences through platforms like GitHub, helping to disseminate innovative solutions and push the state of the art.
- **Interdisciplinary collaboration:**
  The community brings together experts in computer science, ethics, law, and social sciences, facilitating a holistic approach to the challenges posed by AI. This collaboration fosters the development of standards and protocols that integrate both technical and societal aspects.

1.2. User experience feedback

- **Constructive feedback:**
  Users, whether developers integrating the API into their projects or end users interacting with AI-powered applications, provide essential feedback on the performance, relevance, and security of the generated responses.
- **Bug detection and reporting of inappropriate behavior:**
  Feedback from forums and discussion platforms allows for the rapid detection of anomalies or deviations, thus facilitating the implementation of correction and improvement iterations.

2. Specific roles of developers

2.1. Technical contributions and functional extensions

- **Plugin and extension development:**
  Many developers create add-ons that integrate language model functionality into third-party systems (CRM, ERP, collaborative platforms, etc.). These contributions enrich the ecosystem and make the tools more adaptable to various use cases.
- **Performance optimization:**
  The community is working on improving inference algorithms, reducing latency, and optimizing hardware resource utilization. This is evidenced by open source projects dedicated to quantification or fine-tuning specific tasks.

2.2. Development and sharing of practical guides

- **Documentation and tutorials:**
  Developers share guides, tutorials, and technical articles that help new users understand how to effectively integrate and leverage APIs. These educational resources, often available on platforms like GitHub or specialized blogs, accelerate the learning curve.
- **Integration examples and use cases:**
  By sharing code examples and prototype projects, the community provides concrete examples of how to solve common problems, driving adoption and innovation.

---

3. Specific roles of end users

3.1. Feedback and continuous improvement

- **Real-world testing:**
  End users, whether in businesses or individuals, interact with AI-powered applications and provide feedback on the quality of responses, relevance of information, and user-friendliness of interfaces.
- **Identification of specific needs:**
  Their feedback makes it possible to identify use cases not anticipated by developers, opening the way to new functionalities or the adaptation of the tool to specific sectors (customer service, education, health, etc.).

3.2. Reporting problematic content

- **Safety and Ethics Vigilance:**
  Users also help monitor for bias, misinformation, or inappropriate content. Their feedback is crucial for adjusting filters and moderation mechanisms.
- **Participating in support forums:**
  Many users help each other through forums, Reddit communities, or Discord groups, sharing their experiences and advising on how best to formulate prompts or interpret model responses.

4. Forums, collaborative platforms and social networks

4.1. Dedicated discussion spaces

- **Specialized forums:**
  Platforms such as Reddit (with subreddits dedicated to AI), Stack Overflow, and technical forums allow developers and users to discuss problems encountered, ask questions, and propose solutions.
- **Groups on Slack, Discord, or Microsoft Teams:**
  These spaces encourage more informal, real-time exchanges, enabling rapid communication between

community members. Dedicated chat rooms for prompting tips, technical updates, or feedback facilitate the dissemination of knowledge.

4.2. Open source and collaboration platforms

- **GitHub and GitLab:**
  Contributing to open source projects on platforms like GitHub is essential for sharing code, diagnostic tools, and fine-tuning scripts.
- **Blogs and technical articles:**
  Developers and researchers regularly publish articles on Medium, Dev.to or institutional blogs that detail their experiences, the problems encountered and the solutions provided.

---

5. Impact of the community on the evolution of AI technologies

5.1. Acceleration of innovation

- **Idea exchange and rapid iteration:**
  The community allows for rapid testing of new ideas, feedback, and iteration on prototypes. This accelerates the research and development process by providing an environment for continuous experimentation.
- **Influence on updates and roadmaps:**
  User and developer feedback is incorporated into model and API updates. This feedback influences the roadmap, prioritizing features deemed essential by the community.

5.2. Strengthening transparency and trust

- **Open dialogue and process transparency:**
  By openly sharing their work, challenges, and

successes, community members build trust with all
users.
- **Participation in security audits and testing:**
  The community also plays a role in the external
  validation of systems, participating in security tests and
  independent audits that ensure the robustness and ethics
  of the technologies deployed.

6. Conclusion

The developer and user community is a driving force behind
the evolution of artificial intelligence technologies. Through its
role in sharing knowledge, identifying specific needs, and
validating tools, this community contributes to:

- **Accelerate innovation** by facilitating interdisciplinary
  collaboration and rapidly iterating on prototypes,
- **Improving model quality** and safety through
  continuous feedback and open dialogue on technical
  and ethical challenges,
- **Strengthen transparency** and end-user trust by
  making development processes more accessible and
  participatory.

In short, dynamic interaction between developers and users,
supported by forums, collaborative platforms, and social
networks, is essential for creating and maintaining AI systems
that are efficient, responsible, and constantly improving. This
ongoing dialogue allows the ecosystem to adapt to
technological and societal developments, thus ensuring optimal
and ethical use of advances in artificial intelligence.

Infrastructure evolution (update, roadmap, future features).

1. Modernization and updating of technical infrastructure

1.1. Evolution of material resources

- **Increasing computing power:**
  To train increasingly complex and large models, the infrastructure relies on clusters of latest-generation GPUs and TPUs. As scaling increases, vendors are investing in high-performance computing systems capable of processing billions of parameters.
- **Storage and memory optimization:**
  Managing large data sets requires distributed and resilient storage solutions. Network-attached storage (NAS) or cloud-based architectures can efficiently manage the terabytes of data required for training and inference.
- **Hardware innovations:**
  The adoption of technologies such as half-precision computing (FP16 or BF16) and specific optimizations, such as model quantization for inference, reduce resource load and accelerate processing without significant performance loss.

1.2. Optimization of software architectures

- **Advanced parallelism techniques:**
  To distribute training across multiple nodes, methods such as data parallelism, model parallelism, or hybrid techniques (e.g., DeepSpeed's ZeRO) are integrated. These approaches allow training even larger models while optimizing the use of available resources.
- **Open source frameworks and tools:**
  Regular updates of the frameworks used (PyTorch,

TensorFlow, etc.) and the integration of specialized libraries (DeepSpeed, Megatron-LM) ensure that the infrastructure remains at the cutting edge of deep learning techniques and benefits from the latest advances in optimization and scalability.

2. Strategic roadmap and future planning

2.1. Update objectives and new features

- **Performance and stability improvements:**
  The roadmap includes goals to reduce latency, improve context management over long conversations, and optimize convergence during training to increase the model's robustness in real-world conditions.
- **Future features and multimodal extensions:**
  One key direction is the integration of multimodal capabilities. This could include analyzing and generating not only textual content but also visual, audio, or video content, thus providing a richer and more versatile interaction.
- **Enhanced security and alignment:**
  Efforts are planned to integrate more alignment mechanisms (such as "Constitutional AI") and real-time moderation tools, allowing for better control of responses and ensuring responsible use of the model.

2.2. Integration with existing systems

- **Compatibility and scalability:**
  The roadmap includes improving integration through more robust APIs, creating plugins and extensions for third-party platforms (CRM, ERP, collaborative tools, etc.) and optimizing existing workflows.
- **Customization and local adaptation:**
  Tools will be developed to enable fine-grained

customization of the model based on specific business needs. This includes the ability to adjust AI behavior to comply with internal policies or regulations specific to certain sectors or geographic regions.

---

3. Innovations and adaptations to emerging challenges

3.1. Responding to security and ethics needs

- **Updated moderation protocols:**
  To address new challenges of disinformation and malicious use, the infrastructure will be regularly updated with more powerful detection algorithms and more refined moderation rules.
- **Collaboration with the community and regulators:**
  The roadmap includes ongoing partnerships with regulatory bodies, academic institutions, and civil society groups to co-construct evolving ethical standards and security protocols.

3.2. Scalability and cost optimization

- **Energy optimization:**
  The evolution of the infrastructure takes into account energy and environmental constraints, with solutions aimed at reducing electricity consumption (workload optimization, use of green data centers, etc.).
- **Deployment flexibility:**
  Adopting hybrid cloud solutions and virtualization technologies enables rapid deployment of updates and dynamic management of peak demand, ensuring an agile and responsive infrastructure.

4. Long-term development prospects

4.1. Towards a more integrated and collaborative artificial intelligence

- **Connected AI Ecosystem:**
  The roadmap aims to strengthen interconnection between different players in the sector, promoting the sharing of innovations and interdisciplinary collaboration, which will stimulate the creation of ever more comprehensive and integrated solutions.
- **Integration of user feedback:**
  Future evolution of the infrastructure will rely on a continuous feedback system from developers, user companies and end users, to ensure that improvements meet real and evolving market needs.

4.2. Adaptation to technological advances

- **Monitoring hardware and software innovations:**
  The infrastructure will be regularly reviewed to integrate the latest innovations, whether new GPUs, parallelism techniques or algorithmic optimizations.
- **Preparing for future generations of models:**
  In anticipation of the transition to even larger and more complex models, Anthropic is preparing its infrastructure to support next-generation architectures, capable of processing even more diverse and voluminous data.

Conclusion

The evolution of Anthropic's infrastructure, both technically and strategically, is part of a proactive approach aimed at ensuring the performance, security, and scalability of artificial intelligence systems. The roadmap includes:

- Regular updates to take advantage of the latest advances in hardware and software optimization,
- The deployment of new functionalities, particularly in the multimodal and personalization fields,
- Stronger integration with existing systems through robust APIs and modular solutions,
- Continuous adaptation in the face of security, ethics and scalability challenges.

By combining these different areas of development, Anthropic intends not only to improve its existing products but also to anticipate and respond to the future needs of businesses and users, while consolidating its position as a responsible and innovative player in the field of artificial intelligence.

Chapter 9: Prospects and future developments

Expected improvements from Claude: performance, contextual mastery, creativity.

1. Performance Improvements

1.1. Accelerating inference and reducing latency

- **Algorithm optimization:**
  Improving inference algorithms, for example by integrating techniques like FlashAttention or optimizing half-precision calculations (FP16/BF16), helps reduce response time and increase responsiveness during API calls.
- **Advanced Parallelism:**
  Increased use of data and model parallelism strategies makes it easier to distribute the load across multiple GPUs or TPUs, resulting in increased performance without compromising quality.
- **Reduced energy consumption:**
  By optimizing resource management, it is possible to reduce energy consumption during the training and inference phases, while maintaining high performance. This improvement is crucial for the scalability of services in a commercial context.

1.2. Training optimization

- **Advanced fine-tuning techniques:**
  Improving fine-tuning protocols, for example through more refined supervised reinforcement learning (RLHF), helps stabilize training and reduce convergence errors.

- **Continuous updating and incremental learning:**
  Incorporating a regular update process helps keep
  Claude up to date with new knowledge and incorporate
  real-time feedback to correct errors and improve
  accuracy.
- **Adapting to new datasets:**
  By continually expanding and diversifying the training
  corpus, Claude will be able to better handle linguistic
  variations and specific domains, while improving its
  ability to process increasingly complex information.

2. Increased contextual mastery

2.1. Pop-up Window Extension

- **Long-term memory:**
  One current limitation is the limited context window.
  By increasing this window, Claude will be able to
  retain and use a greater amount of information from
  long conversations or large documents, thus improving
  consistency across multiple exchanges.
- **Improved chain-of-thought techniques:**
  Encouraging the model to develop a multi-step chain-
  of-thought approach would help structure the response
  better and maintain internal logic throughout a complex
  dialogue.

2.2. Better management of dynamic context

- **Retention and recall of historical context:**
  More sophisticated mechanisms for memorizing
  relevant information about the history of exchanges
  will allow for long-term consistency by recalling the
  essential elements of past conversations.
- **Contextual adaptability:**
  The ability to adapt the response based on the

immediate and historical context improves interaction by allowing the model to respond in a personalized and precise manner, taking into account the nuances and specificities of each situation.

2.3. Integration of external sources in real time

- **Dynamic knowledge updating:**
  By integrating mechanisms to query external databases or APIs, Claude could update his answers based on the most recent information, thus ensuring greater relevance in a constantly changing context.
- **Deep contextualization:**
  The ability to integrate additional metadata or contextual information (geolocation, temporal data, user profiles) would make it possible to provide more detailed responses adapted to specific contexts.

---

3. Strengthening creativity

3.1. Generation of innovative and varied content

- **Stimulating creativity:**
  By refining text generation techniques, Claude will be able to offer more original and unexpected answers, which is particularly useful in areas such as the creation of marketing, literary or artistic content.
- **Exploring New Narrative Forms:**
  Claude's ability to create complex narratives or scenarios can be enhanced through adjustments to the sampling process, allowing for increased diversity of responses without sacrificing coherence.

3.2. Adaptation to varied styles and tones

- **Stylistic customization:**
  Allowing the user to specify the style, tone, or register of the response, for example by requesting a humorous, formal, or technical approach, makes the model more versatile and creative.
- **Controlling the degree of innovation:**
  Mechanisms for modulating the level of creativity (by adjusting the temperature parameter or using control prompts) allow the right balance between originality and consistency to be found, depending on the specific needs of each task.

3.3. Encouragement of exploration and ideation

- **Assisted Brainstorming:**
  By integrating advanced prompting techniques, Claude could be used as a brainstorming tool, generating ideas, concepts or innovative solutions in various fields.
- **Multidimensional interaction:**
  Improving the model's ability to explore associations of ideas and combine concepts in unexpected ways helps increase its creativity, providing new perspectives that stimulate innovation.

---

4. Synthesis and perspectives

4.1. A holistic approach to improvement

The improvements expected for Claude are not limited to isolated technical optimizations; they are part of a global strategy aimed at making the model faster, more consistent, and more creative. These complementary axes work together to offer an enriched user experience:

- **Performance:** Faster response times, better resource management and increased reliability allow Claude to be used in demanding environments.
- **Contextual Mastery:** An expanded context window and improved reminder mechanisms ensure more consistent interactions over the long term.
- **Creativity:** By stimulating the ability to invent and adapt responses, Claude can become a powerful tool for generating original content and solving complex problems.

4.2. Implications for industrial and creative applications

These improvements will have a significant impact on various sectors:

- In **customer service** , better contextual awareness and faster responses will lead to smoother and more personalized interactions.
- In **marketing and content creation** , increased creativity will help produce original advertising campaigns and content that stands out.
- In education **and** training , the ability to retain and contextualize information will enable more effective and interactive teaching tools to be offered.
- In **professional applications** in general, the combination of performance, contextual coherence and creativity will make Claude particularly suited to solving complex tasks and collaborative innovation.

Conclusion

The improvements expected for Claude include significant progress on three main areas:

1. **Performance** , through inference optimization, resource management and response time reduction.
2. **Contextual mastery** , by expanding the memory window and improving the ability to manage long and complex dialogues.
3. **Creativity** , through the encouragement of the generation of original content and stylistic personalization.

These developments will help make Claude an even more powerful and versatile tool, capable of adapting to the demands of modern applications while delivering a high-quality user experience. The seamless integration of these improvements will push the current boundaries of AI, paving the way for innovative uses and richer interaction between humans and machines.

Claude's potential role in general AI or in specialized AI (medical, legal, etc.).

1. Claude and the General AI

1.1. A versatile model for communication and understanding

- **Linguistic versatility and adaptability:**
  Claude, like other large language models, is trained on huge text corpora covering a variety of domains, allowing it to handle a wide variety of queries. This ability makes it a natural candidate to play a central role in a general AI—an intelligence capable of understanding and generating language as fluently as a human on a variety of topics.
- **Advanced conversational interaction:**
  Thanks to its self-attention mechanisms and Transformer-like architecture, Claude can maintain a coherent dialogue over multiple turns, memorize the context of a conversation, and adapt its responses based on previous exchanges. This type of interaction is fundamental to building AI that assists users in many areas of daily life—from information retrieval to decision support.

1.2. Towards adaptive and evolutionary intelligence

- **Continuous learning and knowledge updating:**
  From a general AI perspective, one of the major challenges is to be able to continuously evolve by integrating new information and refining its understanding of the world. Regular fine-tuning mechanisms, coupled with human feedback strategies, allow Claude to adapt to changes in knowledge and societal contexts.

- **Ability to reason and solve complex problems:**
  Although general AI remains a long-term goal, Claude could be one of the building blocks of systems capable of performing multi-step reasoning, developing creative solutions to unstructured problems, and interacting with other intelligent systems for complex tasks.

---

2. Claude in specialty AI

2.1. Medical fields

2.1.1. Assistance with diagnosis and medical research

- **Medical Record Analysis:**
  Claude can be integrated into medical record management systems to extract relevant information, summarize clinical reports, and help physicians visualize a patient's history.
- **Clinical Decision Support:**
  Based on validated medical databases, Claude could offer suggestions for diagnoses or treatments, while highlighting uncertainties and recommendations to check with a human expert.
- **Research and synthesis of scientific articles:**
  The model can facilitate medical monitoring by synthesizing recent publications, identifying trends or extracting key points from research work, which accelerates innovation and the dissemination of knowledge.

2.1.2. Security and compliance

- **Sensitive Data Privacy:**
  In the medical field, compliance with regulations (such as GDPR in Europe or HIPAA in the United States) is crucial. Claude, by being integrated into secure systems

and applying strict moderation and anonymization protocols, could help preserve confidentiality while offering advanced features.

2.2. Legal areas

2.2.1. Assistance in legal drafting and analysis

- **Drafting documents and contracts:**
  By leveraging his text generation capabilities, Claude can help draft contracts, reformulate clauses to clarify their meaning, or generate administrative documents in compliance with required legal formats.
- **Legal Research:**
  The model can query legal databases and extract information on court precedents, laws or regulations, thus providing support to lawyers in preparing cases and formulating legal strategies.

2.2.2. Compliance verification and risk analysis

- **Auditing legal documents:**
  Claude could be used to detect inconsistencies, errors or risky wording in legal documents, thus helping to prevent potential disputes.
- **Risk Analysis Synthesis:**
  By compiling information from multiple sources, the model can help companies assess legal risks related to specific projects, the implementation of new regulations, or ongoing litigation.

2.3. Other areas of specialization

2.3.1. Finance and economics

- **Financial Report Analysis:**
  Claude can process large amounts of financial data to generate summaries, identify trends and assist in

strategic decision-making in companies or financial institutions.

- **Investment advice:**
  By integrating real-time market data, the model could offer investment recommendations, while specifying that these advice must be validated by financial experts.

2.3.2. Engineering and technology

- **Technical Design and Research Support:**
  In fields such as engineering or technological research, Claude could help synthesize technical documents, generate design ideas, or analyze experience reports.
- **Technical documentation management:**
  The model can automate the writing and updating of specification documents, thus facilitating knowledge transfer within technical teams.

---

3. Specific challenges in specialty AI

3.1. Adaptation to technical contexts

- **Specific Knowledge Areas:**
  To be effective in a specialized field, Claude must be fine-tuned with specific corpora, in order to master the terminology, practices and nuances specific to each sector.
- **Expert validation:**
  In sensitive sectors such as medicine or law, the responses generated must be systematically validated by professionals to avoid errors that could have serious consequences.

3.2. Security and confidentiality

- **Protection of sensitive data:**
  Claude's integration into specialized environments requires reinforced security protocols to protect personal and confidential data, particularly in the medical or legal fields.
- **Regulatory compliance:**
  As each sector is subject to specific regulations, the use of Claude must be accompanied by measures guaranteeing compliance with current standards, which may require technical and operational adaptations.

4. Future prospects

4.1. Towards increased specialization

- **Specific add-ons and plugins:**
  Extensions or dedicated modules could be developed to adapt Claude to the needs of each sector, for example a legal module for drafting and verifying contracts or a medical module for analyzing patient records.
- **Interdisciplinary collaboration:**
  The success of specialty AI requires close collaboration between technical experts and professionals in the relevant sector, allowing for the continuous refinement of the model's performance in specific areas.

4.2. Impact on professions and innovation

- **Automation of repetitive tasks:**
  In each sector, Claude could automate repetitive and time-consuming tasks, freeing up time for professionals to focus on higher value-added activities.
- **Improving the quality of services:**
  By providing accurate answers and synthesizing complex information, the model could improve the

quality of services, whether medical care, legal advice or financial analysis.

- **Driving Innovation:**
  With his creative generation and in-depth analytical skills, Claude can become a partner of choice for innovation in various sectors, helping to identify new opportunities, design innovative solutions and accelerate research and development.

Conclusion

Claude's potential role in both general and specialized AI illustrates an ambition that is both broad and focused. On the one hand, Claude embodies the idea of a versatile conversational intelligence capable of interacting on a multitude of subjects, making it a pillar of general AI. On the other, by specializing and adapting to the requirements of specialized fields such as medicine, law, finance, or engineering, it could become a tailor-made tool capable of providing precise analyses, automating complex tasks, and contributing to improving the quality of services.

Achieving this transition will require specific fine-tuning in each area, ensuring expert validation, and ensuring rigorous compliance with current regulations. In the long term, integrating Claude into specialized environments could not only transform professional practices but also stimulate innovation and improve decision-making in sectors crucial to society.

Anticipation of new challenges (regulations, competition, ethics and governance of AI).

1. Regulations and legal framework

1.1. Evolution of international standards

- **Developing legislative frameworks:**
  Many countries and international organizations (European Union, OECD, UNESCO) are currently working on legal frameworks to govern the development and use of AI. These regulations aim to ensure the security, data protection, and transparency of AI systems.
- **The EU AI Act:**
  The European Union is developing the AI Act, which will be one of the first pieces of legislation to classify AI applications according to their level of risk, imposing strict obligations on systems considered high-risk, such as those used in medicine, law, or finance.

1.2. Compliance and data protection

- **GDPR and Privacy:**
  Regulations such as the General Data Protection Regulation (GDPR) impose constraints on the collection, processing, and storage of personal data. Anticipating privacy requirements is essential for any company developing AI systems.
- **AI System Security:**
  Security requirements aim to prevent malicious use and cyberattacks, leading to enhanced security protocols and regular audits to ensure system integrity.

1.3. Legal liability

- **Liability Allocation:**
  A major issue is determining who is legally liable in the event of AI failure or misuse – the developer, the user company, or both.
- **Insurance and guarantees:**
  Changes in regulations could require the implementation of insurance mechanisms or financial guarantees to cover possible damages linked to the use of AI systems.

---

2. Competition and market dynamics

2.1. Competition between major players

- **Technological rivalry:**
  Companies like OpenAI, Google, Microsoft, Meta, and Anthropic are fiercely competing to develop increasingly powerful and efficient models. This competition drives innovation, but can also lead to a technological arms race, where speed sometimes trumps security and ethics.
- **Patenting and intellectual property:**
  Competition also manifests itself at the intellectual property level, with companies filing patents on key technologies. This dynamic can hamper open collaboration and knowledge exchange.

2.2. New entries and disruptive innovations

- **Startups and open source initiatives:**
  Alongside the tech giants, numerous startups and open source projects are emerging, offering innovative and often more specialized solutions. These players are challenging the status quo and pushing the major players to constantly innovate.

- **Internationalization and global competition:**
  Competition is not limited to Western players.
  Companies and research institutes from countries such
  as China, India, and Japan are investing heavily in AI,
  thus changing the overall market dynamics.

2.3. Commercial pressures and time to market

- **Accelerated development cycle:**
  The pressure to quickly bring powerful AI solutions to
  market can lead to shortcuts in the verification and
  ethics process, increasing the risk of failures or
  malicious use.
- **Differentiation strategies:**
  Each player seeks to distinguish itself through unique
  innovations, whether through superior performance,
  better security or a more advanced ethical approach.

3. Ethics and governance of AI

3.1. Ethical challenges related to bias and misinformation

- **Algorithmic bias:**
  AI systems, trained on large datasets, often reproduce
  the biases present in those data. AI ethics involves
  developing mechanisms to detect, correct, and
  minimize these biases.
- **Disinformation and Manipulation:**
  The potential use of AI to generate and spread
  disinformation is a major challenge. Governments,
  businesses, and researchers must collaborate to develop
  moderation strategies and standards to limit these risks.

3.2. Governance and transparency

- **Shared governance models:**
  AI governance should involve multiple stakeholders, including businesses, regulators, researchers, and civil society. Boards of directors or ethics committees can be established to oversee the development and use of AI.
- **Algorithm Transparency:**
  Making AI models more transparent, by publishing methodologies and implementing interpretability tools, helps build greater trust and ensure greater accountability in the event of deviations.

3.3. Participation of society and public dialogue

- **Public consultations and ethical debates:**
  Public involvement in the AI debate is essential to define acceptable values and boundaries. Discussion forums, public consultations, and cross-sector panels help integrate societal concerns into AI governance.
- **Education and awareness:**
  Training and informing the general public about the challenges of AI, its opportunities and its risks, helps create an environment where decisions are made with full knowledge of the facts, thus promoting a more responsible adoption of the technology.

---

4. Future prospects and anticipatory measures

4.1. Continuous adaptation to technological and societal developments

- **Updating regulatory frameworks:**
  Regulators will need to continually adapt legislation to keep pace with technological innovations, working closely with AI stakeholders to develop flexible and scalable standards.

- **Ethical innovation:**
  AI research and development must incorporate ethical oversight mechanisms, such as model alignment and algorithmic transparency, from the outset to anticipate and reduce negative impacts.

4.2. International collaboration and harmonization of standards

- **Global initiatives:**
  International initiatives, such as those led by the OECD, the EU or UNESCO, aim to establish common standards for the development and use of AI, thus facilitating harmonized governance on a global scale.
- **Public-private partnerships:**
  Cooperation between governments, businesses, and academic institutions is essential to creating robust, responsible, and equitable AI ecosystems. These partnerships can enable the sharing of best practices and the establishment of common regulatory tools.

Conclusion

Anticipating new challenges in the field of artificial intelligence—whether related to regulations, competition, ethics, or governance—is a complex and multifaceted task. Rapid advances in technology require constant updating of legal and ethical frameworks, enhanced international cooperation, and shared governance that involves all stakeholders.

For players like Anthropic, this means not only developing increasingly efficient and secure models, but also anticipating and integrating regulatory developments, addressing competitive challenges, and placing ethics and transparency at the heart of their strategies. By doing so, they are helping to build an environment where AI can develop responsibly, while maximizing its benefits for society and minimizing its potential risks.

Chapter 10: Conclusion and review of societal impact

Summary of the key points covered in the book.

1. Historical Context of Artificial Intelligence

- **The Beginnings of AI:**
  The book traces the beginnings of artificial intelligence, from the ideas of Alan Turing and cybernetics to the first implementations of symbolic systems such as the Logic Theorist and the General Problem Solver.
- **The major milestones:**
  It covers the evolution of approaches, from symbolism to neural networks, through periods of disillusionment called "AI winters" and the subsequent emergence of deep learning.

2. Emergence of Neural Networks and Deep Learning

- **Theoretical Foundations and Key Innovations:**
  The book explores the evolution from Rosenblatt's perceptron to the major advances in backpropagation and deep network architectures that have revolutionized image recognition and natural language processing.
- **Impact on current research:**
  The importance of optimization, distributed computing and advanced parallelism techniques is put into perspective to explain how these technical advances have enabled the rise of models like Claude.

3. Major Actors and Foundation of Anthropic

- **AI Pioneers:**
  The book introduces the iconic figures such as Turing, McCarthy, Minsky, Simon, and Judea Pearl, who laid the foundations of artificial intelligence, as well as the academic labs and companies that shaped the field.
- **Birth of Anthropic:**
  The story of Anthropic's creation is explored, emphasizing its founders' commitment to putting security, ethics, and the alignment of AI systems at the heart of their mission.

4. Philosophy, Vision and Values of Anthropic

- **Ethical Commitment:**
  The book details Anthropic's vision, which aims to develop AI that is aligned with human values, transparent, and responsible.
- **Technical Priorities and Approaches:**
  The use of Constitutional AI and advanced moderation techniques to ensure that models, like Claude, produce safe and balanced responses.

5. Featured Projects and Products: Claude

- **Introducing Claude:**
  The book describes Claude as a large language model based on the Transformer architecture, designed to be a general-purpose conversational assistant.
- **Technical Specifics and Use Cases:**
  It highlights the technical challenges, optimizations (learning rate, bias filtering, attention mechanisms),

and practical applications of Claude in various industries such as customer service, writing, education, etc.

6. Technical Challenges and Future Improvements

- **Training and Datasets:**
  The process of collecting, filtering, and training models is examined in depth, along with optimization techniques and resource consumption management.
- **Current limitations and prospects for improvement:**
  Issues such as hallucinations, context management and sensitivity to formulations are discussed, as well as planned areas of improvement to improve the performance, creativity and robustness of the systems.

7. Applications and Task Automation

- **Concrete examples of applications:**
  The book presents how Claude can transform workflows in various sectors – from the automation of administrative tasks to specialized assistance in fields such as medicine, law or finance.
- **Integration into existing systems:**
  It also discusses the importance of integration via APIs and collaborations with other tools to optimize productivity and efficiency of business processes.

8. Governance, Transparency and Societal Impact

- **Security and Ethics Policies:**
  Emphasis is placed on the need to establish rigorous protocols to prevent malicious use of AI and to promote responsible governance.
- **Community Dialogue:**
  The book highlights the importance of partnerships with the scientific community, regulators, and the public to create a collaborative and transparent environment that guides the future development of AI technologies.

---

9. Roadmap and Future Perspectives

- **Infrastructure Evolution:**
  An overview of planned improvements in performance, scalability and integration with other systems is presented, while anticipating future challenges (regulations, competition, security).
- **General AI vs. Specialty AI:**
  The book considers Claude's future role, both in a general AI approach and in specialty applications that require specific expertise, such as in the medical, legal, or financial fields.

---

10. Conclusion and Overall Impact

- **Summary of the issues:**
  The book concludes by summarizing how the evolution of artificial intelligence, through initiatives such as those of Anthropic and Claude, lays the foundations for

a future where AI will not only be more efficient but also more ethical and responsible.

- **Vision for the future:**
  It invites reflection on the societal impact of AI technologies and the need to pursue interdisciplinary research to ensure that these tools benefit society as a whole, while minimizing potential risks.

This summary synthesizes all the key points covered in the book, providing an overview of the historical, technical, and ethical evolution of artificial intelligence, while illustrating Claude's place and potential in this constantly evolving landscape. Each of these themes combines to offer a comprehensive vision that guides not only the current development, but also the future directions of responsible AI.

How Claude and Anthropic are transforming our relationship with technology.

1. A human-centered approach

1.1. Priority to safety and ethics

- **Alignment with human values:**
  Unlike some companies that focus solely on raw performance, Anthropic integrates a set of ethical principles from the design stage of its systems. The "Constitutional AI" approach aims to ensure that Claude does not generate harmful content, while respecting standards of transparency and accountability.
- **Risk Reduction:**
  By implementing advanced filtering mechanisms and moderation protocols, Anthropic seeks to minimize the risks of misinformation, bias, and malicious use. This focus on security creates a technological environment where users feel protected and can interact with AI with confidence.

1.2. A more intuitive and accessible interaction

- **Natural conversational interfaces:**
  Claude, as a large conversational language model, offers a fluid and accessible interaction that resembles human communication. This facilitates the adoption of AI technologies by a non-specialist audience, transforming complex tools into intelligent assistants accessible to all.
- **Personalization and adaptability:**
  Claude's ability to adapt its responses based on context and user profile allows for personalized experiences. Whether it's customer support, writing assistance, or

tutoring, this flexibility is transforming the way we use technology every day.

---

2. Transformation of professional and personal environments

2.1. Automation and productivity gains

- **Business process optimization:**
  Across diverse sectors—from administration to finance, healthcare, and legal—Claude's integration automates repetitive tasks, generates accurate summaries, and optimizes workflows. This frees up time to focus on higher-value activities, transforming traditional ways of working.
- **New collaboration tools:**
  The use of virtual assistants and intelligent APIs facilitates internal and external communication, enabling better coordination between teams and faster decision-making.

2.2. Impact on learning and innovation

- **Educational Transformation:**
  In the educational field, Claude serves as a teaching support tool, capable of popularizing complex concepts and supporting students in their learning. AI thus becomes a valuable complement to traditional teaching methods, promoting a more interactive education tailored to individual needs.
- **Stimulating Creativity and Research:**
  As a creative assistant, Claude helps generate new ideas, explore innovative avenues, and synthesize information from multiple sources. This role as a catalyst for creativity transforms the way professionals

and researchers approach challenges, paving the way
for new discoveries.

---

3. A societal and cultural transformation

3.1. Democratization of access to AI

- **Accessible and user-friendly tools:**
  Claude's ease of use allows a wide audience, including
  those without in-depth technical knowledge, to benefit
  from advances in artificial intelligence. This
  democratization helps bridge the digital divide and
  promote more equitable adoption of innovative
  technologies.
- **Involvement in daily life:**
  Virtual assistants powered by Claude are increasingly
  integrated into mobile applications, online services and
  even connected devices, thus changing the way we
  interact with technology on a daily basis.

3.2. Dialogue and participatory governance

- **Transparency and collaboration:**
  Anthropic encourages open dialogue with the scientific
  community, regulators, and the public. This sharing of
  information and experiences contributes to a better
  understanding of the challenges of AI and promotes the
  co-construction of ethical and regulatory standards.
- **Collective accountability:**
  By involving diverse stakeholders – researchers,
  businesses, users, and government bodies – in AI
  governance, Anthropic helps establish a technology
  development model where responsibility is shared and
  everyone has a voice.

4. Challenges and future prospects

4.1. Anticipating technological developments

- **Continuous innovation:**
  The rapid evolution of AI technologies means that
  Claude and similar systems will need to constantly
  adapt to new discoveries and advances in
  infrastructure, optimization, and interaction. This
  dynamic encourages a culture of continuous
  improvement and open innovation.
- **Towards a general and specialized AI:**
  While Claude is already positioned as a versatile tool,
  future prospects envisage increased specialization in
  specific fields (medical, legal, financial) while
  continuing the development of a general AI capable of
  handling an infinite variety of subjects with ever-
  increasing precision.

4.2. Responding to ethical and societal challenges

- **Regulation and governance:**
  With evolving legal frameworks and rising ethical
  concerns, it will be crucial to put in place robust
  mechanisms to regulate the use of AI. Anthropic, as a
  pioneer in responsible AI, is well-positioned to
  influence these processes and serve as a model for the
  entire industry.
- **Adapting to new social expectations:**
  The transformation of our relationship with technology
  is not limited to technical advances; it also includes the
  way we perceive and interact with AI. By promoting
  transparency, security, and ethics, Claude and
  Anthropic are helping to establish a technological
  culture where innovation is used to serve the common
  good.

Conclusion

Claude and Anthropic are transforming our relationship with technology by redefining standards for interaction, security, and ethics in the field of artificial intelligence. Their approach, which prioritizes transparency, alignment with human values, and interdisciplinary collaboration, enables us to:

- **Make AI more accessible and user-friendly,** by facilitating interaction with intelligent tools that meet real user needs.
- **Optimize business environments** by automating complex tasks and improving decision-making through accurate and contextual analyses.
- **Foster open dialogue and participatory governance,** involving the scientific community, regulators and the general public to ensure that AI development is carried out in a responsible and ethical manner.
- **Anticipate and adapt to technological developments,** continually innovating to meet future challenges while integrating advanced security and moderation mechanisms.

In short, Anthropic's approach and Claude's development offer a model of technological innovation that puts humans at the center. This transforms our relationship with technology by providing us with powerful tools while encouraging us to rethink the ethical and societal implications of artificial intelligence for a safer and more inclusive future.

Thoughts and ideas for the future: how responsible AI can shape society.

1. Foundations of responsible AI

1.1. Definition and principles of responsible AI

- **Transparency and explainability:**
  Responsible AI must be understandable to its users. The algorithms and decisions made by these systems must be explainable and auditable to ensure trust and enable external verification.
- **Security and robustness:**
  The security of AI systems involves protection against malicious use, failures, and errors. Moderation mechanisms, robustness testing, and regular audits are essential to prevent potential abuses.
- **Fairness and bias reduction:**
  This involves designing systems that minimize algorithmic bias and treat all social groups fairly. This involves careful selection of training data, fine-tuning with human feedback, and the use of debiasing techniques.
- **Accountability and governance:**
  Responsible AI involves shared governance between developers, regulators, and civil society to ensure that decisions made by AI systems are aligned with ethical values and that accountability is clearly assigned in the event of errors.

2. Avenues for reflection for the future of responsible AI

2.1. Governance and regulation

- **Evolving legislative frameworks:**
  One of the major challenges is to implement flexible regulations that can keep pace with technological advances. Laws like the AI Act in Europe are examples. These regulations must protect citizens while not hampering innovation.
- **Multi-stakeholder participation:**
  AI governance must involve all stakeholders –

governments, businesses, researchers, NGOs, and citizens – to create shared standards that ensure the ethical and safe use of AI technologies.

2.2. Technological development and responsible innovation

- **Human-centered design:**
  The future of AI must be shaped by approaches that integrate user needs and expectations. Intuitive interfaces, personalized assistance systems, and collaborative tools can transform how we interact with technology.
- **Transparency in research and development:**
  Encouraging the publication of methodologies, research results, and independent audits helps build trust. Open source initiatives and cross-sector research consortia promote the dissemination of best practices.

2.3. Societal and ethical impact

- **Bridging the digital divide:**
  Responsible AI must be accessible to all to reduce technological inequalities. This includes democratizing access to AI tools and training citizens on their use.
- **Promoting inclusion and diversity:**
  AI systems should be designed to reflect diverse cultures and opinions. By minimizing bias and adapting technologies to the specific needs of communities, AI can become a vehicle for social justice.
- **Supporting careers and transforming work:**
  Intelligent and responsible automation can free individuals from repetitive and dangerous tasks, while creating new job opportunities in innovative sectors. However, it is crucial to plan reskilling and training programs to support this transition.

2.4. Issues of disinformation and manipulation

- **Proactive moderation:**
  Responsible AI systems incorporate advanced filtering and moderation mechanisms to limit the spread of misinformation. Techniques such as Constitutional AI and human feedback reinforcement help control the quality of generated content.
- **Media literacy:**
  Alongside powerful technological tools, it is essential to educate the public on source verification and critical understanding of content disseminated by AI systems. This will strengthen society's resilience against manipulation.

3. Future scenarios and prospective visions

3.1. Integrated AI in all sectors

- **Healthcare, education, finance, law, the environment:**
  Responsible AI could transform many sectors by providing tailor-made solutions adapted to the specific requirements of each field. For example, in healthcare, it could help diagnose diseases early and personalize treatments, while in education, it could offer personalized and interactive learning.
- **Smooth and natural interaction:**
  Integrating AI into daily life will improve quality of life, offering virtual assistants capable of understanding context, memorizing interaction history and providing precise and personalized advice.

3.2. International collaboration for a common future

- **Global standardization:**
  International cooperation is essential to develop common standards that govern the development of AI,

in order to avoid a technological arms race and ensure fair use globally.

- **Collaborative research and shared innovation:** Cross-sector consortia and partnerships will foster the co-construction of innovative solutions, combining technical, ethical, and societal expertise. This will help address challenges holistically and ensure that AI serves the common good.

3.3. Reflections on general AI and the limits of the machine

- **Towards augmented intelligence:** The future could see the emergence of an AI that is not simply autonomous but works in synergy with humans, augmenting intellectual and creative abilities rather than replacing them.
- **Existential and philosophical questions:** The rise of AI raises fundamental questions about the nature of consciousness, the moral responsibility of machines, and the very definition of intelligence. These reflections, far from being purely theoretical, will guide the evolution of technologies so that they remain in line with human values.

4. Conclusion

Anticipating new challenges in the field of responsible AI represents a technical, ethical, and societal challenge. For artificial intelligence to positively shape the future, it is essential to:

- **Establish flexible regulatory frameworks** that protect citizens while encouraging innovation,

- **Developing transparent and explainable AI systems,** capable of integrating advanced security mechanisms and reducing bias,
- **Promote collaborative governance,** involving all stakeholders – governments, businesses, researchers and the general public – to co-construct universal ethical standards,
- **Support inclusion and education,** so that all citizens can understand and benefit from advances in AI,
- **Promote research and open innovation,** so that AI becomes a tool for increasing human capabilities rather than a source of inequality or manipulation.

By adopting this multifaceted approach, responsible AI can truly transform our society by improving quality of life, stimulating innovation, and ensuring technological development that is in harmony with human values. The future of AI, shaped by responsible initiatives, paves the way for a more inclusive, equitable, and resilient society facing the challenges of the 21st century.

Figures and statistics

1. Training data and volumes

- **Data volume** :
  Modern large language models, such as GPT-3, have
  been trained on approximately **45 terabytes** of raw text
  data, after filtering, which represents billions of web
  pages, scientific articles, books, and various content.
- **Tokens Used** :
  For example, GPT-3 was reportedly exposed to over
  300 billion tokens during its pre-training, while next-
  generation models (like GPT-4 or Claude) aim for even
  higher volumes to cover a broader spectrum of
  knowledge.

---

2. Model settings

- **Model sizes** :
  - **GPT-3** has about **175 billion parameters** .
  - **GPT-4** is expected to contain an even larger
    number of parameters, often estimated at
    between **500 billion and** 1 trillion, to improve
    language understanding and reasoning ability.
  - Specialized models developed by Anthropic,
    such as Claude, would fall on a similar scale, or
    even slightly different depending on
    optimization and focus on security/alignment.

---

3. Performance and response time

- **Inference time** :
  Advances in optimization (use of GPU/TPU, half-
  precision calculation, parallelism) now make it possible

to obtain response times of the order of **a few milliseconds to a few seconds** to generate a response, even for complex queries in a commercial environment.

- **Performance Improvement** :
Using techniques such as FlashAttention and the ZeRO model can increase training speed by 2 to 3 times compared to traditional methods, while significantly reducing memory consumption.

4. Economic and market impact

- **AI Market Growth** :
According to various studies, the global artificial intelligence market is expected to reach **$190 billion** by 2025, growing at a compound annual growth rate (CAGR) of over **40%** .

- **AI Investments** :
Investments in AI startups and academic research now exceed **$10 billion annually** globally, indicating the scale and momentum of this growing sector.

5. Adoption and use in businesses

- **Task Automation** :
Across several industries (finance, healthcare, customer service), AI-powered automation has reduced operational costs by **20-30%** and increased productivity by an average of **15-25%** .

- **Integration into customer service** :
By adopting chatbots based on advanced language models, some companies have seen a reduction in customer support wait time of up to **50%** , and an increase in customer satisfaction of **10 to 20 points** on standardized satisfaction indices.

6. Societal and ethical impacts

- **Bias Reduction** :
  Studies show that proper bias management in datasets can reduce treatment disparities in AI systems by **30 to 50%** , depending on the domains and the filtering methods applied.
- **Consumer adoption** :
  According to some surveys, more than **60%** of users are in favor of using virtual assistants in their daily lives, provided that data privacy and security are guaranteed.

These figures and statistics provide insight into the scale of the technical and economic challenges, as well as the potential impact of AI in various fields. They help us understand why players like Anthropic and models like Claude are positioning themselves as pioneers in a rapidly evolving industry, aiming to offer not only cutting-edge performance, but also responsible solutions aligned with ethical values.

www.ingramcontent.com/pod-product-compliance
Lightning Source LLC
LaVergne TN
LVHW051322050326
832903LV00031B/3308